W9-DEA-393

Cost-Effective
Marketing Research

Recent Titles from Quorum Books

Exceptional Entrepreneurial Women: Strategies for Success
Russel R. Taylor

Collective Bargaining and Impasse Resolution in the Public Sector
David A. Dilts and William J. Walsh

New Directions in MIS Management: A Guide for the 1990s
Robert J. Thierauf

The Labor Lawyer's Guide to the Rights and Responsibilities of
Employee Whistleblowers
Stephen M. Kohn and Michael D. Kohn

Strategic Organization Planning: Downsizing for Survival
David C. Dougherty

Joint Venture Partner Selection: Strategies for Developed Countries
J. Michael Geringer

Sustainable Corporate Growth: A Model and Management Planning
Tool
John J. Clark, Thomas C. Chiang, and Gerard T. Olson

Competitive Freedom Versus National Security Regulation
Manley Rutherford Irwin

Labor Law and Business Change: Theoretical and Transactional
Perspectives
Samuel Estreicher and Daniel G. Collins, eds.

The Constitutional Right to a Speedy and Fair Criminal Trial
Warren Freedman

Entrepreneurial Systems for the 1990s: Their Creation, Structure,
and Management
John E. Tropman and Gersh Morningstar

From Organizational Decline to Organizational Renewal: The
Phoenix Syndrome
Mary E. Guy

Modern Analytical Auditing: Practical Guidance for Auditors and
Accountants
Thomas E. McKee

Multiple Use Job Descriptions: A Guide to Analysis, Preparation, and
Applications for Human Resources Managers
Philip C. Grant

Cost-Effective Marketing Research

A GUIDE FOR MARKETING MANAGERS

Eric J. Soares

Q

QUORUM BOOKS

New York
Westport, Connecticut
London

Library of Congress Cataloging-in-Publication Data

Soares, Eric J.
　Cost–effective marketing research : a guide for marketing managers
　/ Eric J. Soares.
　　p.　cm.
　Bibliography: p.
　Includes index.
　ISBN 0–89930–278-5 (lib. bdg. : alk. paper)
　1. Marketing research.　I. Title.
HF5415.2.S63　1988
658.8'3—dc19　　88–18526

British Library Cataloguing in Publication Data is available.

Library of Congress Catalog Card Number: 88–18526
ISBN: 0–89930–278-5

First published in 1988 by Quorum Books

Greenwood Press, Inc.
88 Post Road West, Westport, Connecticut　06881

Printed in the United States of America

The paper used in this book complies with the
Permanent Paper Standard issued by the National
Information Standards Organization (Z39.48-1984).

10　9　8　7　6　5　4　3　2　1

Contents

Preface   vii

Acknowledgments   xi

1. What Marketing Research Is Good For   1

2. Using Secondary Information   13

3. Surveying   25

4. Depth Interviews and Focus Groups   51

5. Observation   69

6. Experimentation   81

7. Data Analysis   109

8. Reporting Results   137

References   153

Index   161

Preface

I am a business man, consultant, and professor. As for my business, I am president of Tsunami Products, a manufacturer of sea kayaks. My consulting activities involve sales training and marketing research for small and medium-size businesses. As of this writing, I have consulted with twenty-six organizations. I am also an adjunct marketing research director for THOMAS RAHM Advertising and Public Relations of Oakland, California. As an associate professor, I teach graduate and undergraduate marketing research courses at California State University at Hayward. I also teach marketing management, business communication, and sales personnel training and development. I am also a well-known name in the world of sea kayaking.

Business is a lot like sea kayaking. Good decisions are essential in both activities. A bad business decision can cost you a lot of money; a bad kayaking decision can cost you your life. Accurate, timely, and relevant information helps business people and kayakers make good decisions they can commit to—with confidence. This book shows you how to get good information to make good decisions and how to do it inexpensively.

My aim is to describe efficient and useful marketing research methods to help marketing managers obtain and use pertinent information to make sound decisions. Tips and rules of thumb guide you through the complex maze of research techniques to find the best way to tackle your information needs. This book is a concise, pragmatic manual that pinpoints the quickest, leanest way to get needed information. Abstract theories and capricious methods are pushed aside in favor of parsimonious, proven, and innovative ways of knowing.

The book is organized into eight chapters. The first chapter delineates the role of research in your decision-making process. The question "Do we need research?" is answered. How much research is needed, who should do it, and how they should do it are addressed. I outline each major step in the research process.

The second chapter discusses the utility and pitfalls of using secondary (already published) data and syndicated research. A no-nonsense approach to surveying is the focus of Chapter three, in which I discuss the best data collection methods, how to put together and pilot test questionnaires, ways to determine sample size and selection, and how to conduct the survey. Also covered are how to avoid, overcome, or minimize survey errors.

In Chapter four, the proper uses of depth interview and focus group techniques are described. Chapter five centers on ethnography and quantitative, systematic observation of behavior. Chapter six covers experimentation, the queen of marketing research methods. Experimentation is presented as the ultimate way to assess causal relationships and test the marketing mix. I provide methods, tips, and rules of thumb when experimenting.

Ways of editing, analyzing, and interpreting data comprise Chapter seven, which deals with topics such as the use and misuse of statistics. Qualitative and quantitative data analysis considerations are discussed, including multivariate statistics. I describe classic and current software packages available for mainframe and personal computers. The final chapter describes how to persuasively translate research findings into usable input for rational decisions. I show you how to put together a top-notch research report and guide you to effective oral presentation of research findings. I also discuss current business competition and marketing research ethics.

In short, this book is a practical, efficient guide to research methods for marketing managers, research practitioners, and entrepreneurs. I put my experience as a research consultant, executive, and professor into the book. I also include findings and experience of other research professionals and offer titles of classic and innovative articles and books to enhance your knowledge in specialty areas. I voice my opinion and provide rules of thumb in areas such as sample size, focus group moderating, observing behavior, experimental designs, editing data, statistical software, and writing reports. I have taken every reasonable precaution to ensure accuracy and soundness in my recommendations. However, I take full responsibility for my opinions, errors, and omissions.

The way to get the most cost-effective use out of this book is to read it through once. Then refer to specific chapters as the need arises as you address company research concerns. This book will have served its purpose if it helps you make one marketing decision that saves or earns your company money. My research shows that it will.

Acknowledgments

As with every book, there are many people who contribute directly or indirectly to the finished product. I thank Lisa Campbell for her support in me and the project. I thank Tom Gannon of Quorum for being such an understanding editor. I thank Judith Mason for her library research and help in preparing the manuscript.

Several scholars taught me much of the research I know. I give thanks again to Larry Chase for inspiring me to learn how to learn, for power analysis and for those first consulting opportunities. I thank these people for teaching me research methods from many fields: Tony Mulac for structured observation; Don Zimmerman for ethnomethodology and conversation analysis; John Wiemann for methods of studying nonverbal behavior; Val Smith for computer statistical packages and data analysis; Gene Knepprath for survey research and sampling; Fred Pigge for descriptive and inferential statistics; Susan Parrish for multiple regression; Jim Solomon for voice pitch analysis; Gil Frisbie for marketing research applications, and Carol

Shuherk for participant observation and depth inter-viewing.

I thank Raymond K. Tucker for experimental design and multivariate statistics. Dr. Tucker taught me how to contribute to life. I humbly extend my gratitude.

Cost-Effective
Marketing Research

1

What Marketing Research Is Good For

What marketing decisions are you making today? Suppose your company has developed a prototype of a new product. Before they spend millions producing and marketing this product, your superiors want to know certain information beforehand. First, they want to know if there is demand for the product, and how much? And if none, can demand be created, and how? They want to know how much consumers like the idea of their new product, and which features potential buyers want. They want to know demographics, attributes, and buying patterns of these consumers—and how many there are. They want to know who the competition is and whether they have comparable products on the market or in development. If comparable products exist, which is better, yours or theirs? What is the market share for their products? What is the potential share for yours? Can the market be expanded? By how much? How? If this product were produced in limited quantities, how would you test its salability and marketing mix variables? If the product were produced for max-

imum distribution, how would you package and price it?
On what information would you base these decisions?
What would the sales of this product be in the first year?
The second? What governmental and legal considerations
will influence the development of this product? These and
hundreds more questions could and should be asked of a
marketing manager. One final question: How much is it
going to cost to get the information to help make decisions
about this proposed new product?

There is no question that marketing research is needed
to help make rational decisions. By rational, I refer to
decisions based on a combination of intuition, experience,
expert opinion, and good information, not impulse or
programmed decisions. Rational decisions need to be
made in times of uncertainty, when problems or opportunities arise. This book is concerned with the "good information" part of decision making. Good information costs
money. But how much? This chapter outlines steps in the
research process, how much research costs, who to use to
do the research, and how to choose the right people.

STEPS IN THE RESEARCH PROCESS

There are ten steps in the marketing research process.
Most of these steps are covered in varying degrees in standard marketing research texts (for example, see Dillon,
Madden, & Firtle 1987; Hartley, Prough, & Flaschner
1983; Kinnear & Taylor 1987; Parasuraman 1986; Peterson 1982; Zikmund 1986). But briefly, here are the ten
steps:

1. Identify needs—problems or opportunities—and state research objectives.
2. Examine historical data and conduct exploratory studies.
3. Do a cost/benefit analysis—decide if and how much further

research is needed, who should do it, and how it should be done.

4. Develop data collection forms and methods—if further research is mandated.
5. Layout data analysis plan—figure out how data will be analyzed and interpreted.
6. Select sample.
7. Collect data.
8. Process data.
9. Analyze and interpret data.
10. Present findings.

These steps are discussed in subsequent chapters. For now, let us turn to the first three steps. The first involves identifying needs. This step is inexpensive and involves discussing problems and opportunities with appropriate colleagues to reach consensus as to what needs to be done to address the issues. Although this is the easiest step in theory, in practice it is often the most difficult. The reason? Many marketing managers experience resistance from seniors and peers in other divisions. It is not the purpose of this book to bemoan interpersonnel strife within organizations or to provide answers to conflict. However, you must strive to nurture good working relationships with your colleagues or you will not be able to capitalize on the material presented in this book.

Step 1 is potentially the easiest and the most crucial step in the research process. It is essential to correctly determine research needs, otherwise all subsequent information gathering and decision making will be systematically invalid, resulting in egregious errors. By accurately pinpointing specific research objectives in the initial research process, you will save money and time in the short and long run. The ideal decision-making process goes like this: After the need is felt, team members define the problem/opportunity and list alternatives. Alternatives are evaluated, and one is selected and implemented. This is simple. If the alternative selected is research, then you will have to gather preliminary data to decide how much and what kind of research to conduct. This brings us to the next step.

Once you and your people have identified needs and have listed specific research objectives, you can proceed with step 2, examining historical data and conducting exploratory research. This step resembles step 4, which focuses on designing the research method to gather data. But step 2 is preliminary, quick, and cheap. The idea behind it is to gather enough information to decide if further research is necessary. Thus, the first step is to examine historical resources (secondary data) for information that will contribute to your research objectives and perhaps answer some of your preliminary questions. Secondary data (explained more fully in the following chapter) are found in your company files or computers and in libraries. Secondary data consist of past studies you or others have conducted plus other pertinent information you have filed away.

Step 2 also encompasses some inexpensive exploratory research that will provide an indication of what you may find with more complex descriptive and causal studies. Exploratory research may involve talking to experts, conducting a focus group (see Chapter 4), or pilot surveying a few respondents. As with using secondary research, exploratory studies should be quick and inexpensive. Information obtained in step 2 can serve as a basis to conduct step 3, a cost/benefit analysis.

COST/BENEFIT ANALYSIS

Some type of cost/benefit analysis must be conducted. In unprogrammed marketing decisions, uncertainty is rampant. Marketing mix variables constitute the only controllable factors. Competition, government regulations, and the economy are not controllable. Thus perfect information cannot be obtained to make decisions using mathematical models. However, the value of the research needs to be determined. On the most basic level, benefits of information must outweigh costs.

A few rules of thumb about the value of information follow. First, research value increases with market size and share. So, if there is a lot of money to be made, it pays to conduct research, even extensive and expensive research. This axiom is particularly true if the decision contains a large degree of uncertainty. In a large market where your company stands to gain a lot of money, you hardly need to calculate a break-even point on the cost of your research. An armchair evaluation should quickly and decisively determine the benefits of research. The key point is to avoid spending large amounts of time and human resources debating the obvious.

Information from research is needed in a small market also, so when determining the value of research, keep the cost of research down. Be judicious in selecting the type and extent of research. Do not even consider expensive ways to get information. Refer to subsequent chapters in this book to figure out how you can cost effectively get good data.

In summary, the value of research must be determined. Large markets with large market share are classical targets for marketing research. But even small markets and small market share deserve research. In both cases, smart marketing managers will figure out which methods provide the most information for the least amount of cost.

DETERMINING WHO SHOULD CONDUCT THE STUDY

To calculate the overall cost of research, you must cost out alternatives in each of the remaining steps in the research process. The first and most important cost element is selecting the proper people to conduct the research. This boils down to two choices: in-house or outside.

Using In-house Researchers

If research is conducted in-house, you, someone in your department or another division, or your research department must do it. You can do it (or lead your staff) if you are qualified. Here is what constitutes qualified: you must have taken research, data analysis, and statistics courses or workshops. Without the breadth and depth of systematic study of research methods, you will be limited in what you can apply. You will exemplify the "boy with a hammer" who uses it across all situations because it is all he has. You should also have taken part in previous studies so you possess experience to back up your knowledge.

How do you get the requisite education and experience? Most undergraduate marketing majors today take marketing research, statistics, and data base management classes. But I have found that many of my MBA students have had no research courses at all. The good news is that future marketing managers will have basic research skills; the bad news is that many current marketing professionals do not. If you fall into the have not or not enough category, there is a straightforward remedy. Take marketing research at a local university. Or enroll in a comprehensive marketing research seminar through the American Marketing Association (AMA) or a private research firm. Many university courses require research projects as an integral part of the class. In addition to the aforementioned, you should also read many of the books and publications that are noted throughout this book. These courses and reading materials will increase your competence in marketing research. Taking these courses is essential if you are involved in a new venture and wear many hats. However, there are caveats to heed if you are considering leading the research project.

Being qualified does not necessarily make you the ideal person for the job. You may have too many other responsibilities to give marketing research projects the close supervision they need. Also, your staff may not have the skills, time, or resources to complete the task. Another problem centers around your personal investment in the outcome of the study. If you are too subjective, for whatever the reason, you are not the ideal person for the job. Maybe someone else in your company should do it. You could use personnel from another department. But the same problems may surface, so be aware of their skills and vested interests in the outcome of the study.

If your company is large enough to employ a research staff, these people will be likely candidates to conduct the research. There are benefits to using in-house research personnel. The first benefit is they are on call to do company research, so your work will keep them busy. In fact, their presence alone makes it more likely that the research will be conducted. Top management will likely see the value of using available human resources. Second, because they are in-house, it would likely be cheaper to use them instead of some outside research firm. Unless they are unusually busy, it is probable they could conduct the research faster than an outside agency could. Probably the best reason to use your company research team is they know the company, its history, products, and culture. There is no learning curve to figure into the costs and time line.

Unfortunately, the most important reason to use in-house people is also the most important reason not to use them. They may be too involved with company politics and research outcomes. They may be myopic in some ways. Unique facilities, specialists, or equipment may not be available to suit the best research method. Finally, it may be a waste of money to keep a full-time staff on call, unless they are used often or perform collateral duties.

There are other in-house alternatives to conducting the research yourself or employing a full-time staff. You could hire researchers part-time or subcontract with specific researchers whenever they are needed. This would be more cost effective, yet ensure that the researchers were familiar with your organization and its characteristics.

Using Outside Research Firms

Even if you are capable of doing the research and have a research department, you may still wish to consider employing an outside research firm. The benefits are many. First, outside firms are likely to be more objective than your researchers because they have no personal involvement in the outcome of the research. Second, they may be cheaper. Outside firms are very competitive with each other and have developed efficient and proprietary ways of conducting just the type of research you may need.

Another good reason to seek the help of research companies is that they may be uniquely qualified to conduct your research. Their personnel, facilities, and equipment may be dedicated for specialty research—such as focus groups, mechanical observation, telephone research, or test marketing. More and more research firms specialize in particular methods, and there are more firms to choose from than in the past. As an example, the San Francisco area features over 100 marketing research firms. If your business were located there, you would have plenty of research organizations to choose from. My recommendation: if you have no research personnel or if the research questions demand outside help—get it.

Do be wary, however. Problems exist when using outside researchers. First, it may be a hassle choosing the right company. At the least, valuable time is used obtaining good research help. Then more time (and money) is gobbled up as the agency learns about your company and its information needs. Finally, the biggest potential problem area lies in the trustworthiness of the company. Can you be sure if the method, analysis, and results are right? You cannot oversee every step of their work. You have to trust that their "proprietary" methods are sound, that surveyors are accurate and honest, that data editing and entry errors were avoided, that correct and appropriate statistics were used, and that the entire process was done ethically and efficiently, with your company's best interests at heart. According to Stern and Crawford (1986: 20), the marketing research field, unlike accounting and law, has no certification program to ensure minimum competencies of its practitioners. The loser is you. So, until certification is no longer an issue, the research consumer must exercise caution when selecting research firms.

Here are some suggestions to make sure your experiences with outside agencies are good ones. First, if you have a good working relationship with an outside firm, use them or ask them to refer you to someone they trust. If you have no experience using outside firms or simply wish to get the best deal for your money, solicit proposals from relevant agencies listed in the telephone directory, with the chamber of commerce, or the American Marketing Association. But do your homework. Know specifically what and who you are looking for. A number of authors have provided tips on selecting research consultants (see Flegal 1983; Pope 1980; Smith 1980; Tauber 1981; Townsend 1986). You should check your library to read their advice. My advice is presented here. When soliciting for researchers, use the shotgun approach. Mail requests for proposals (rfp's) to all qualified firms. Then select the best one based on criteria listed in your rfp.

Here is what an rfp should contain. A transmittal letter

leads the request to cue the company as to what you are asking for in the rfp. The rfp proper includes a concise statement of the problem and a request for bids. Background on the problem follows. Include enough relevant information about the history and current status of your information needs so a research company can give you a detailed proposal that addresses nuances, not just the general need. Describe all details you have on how you think the problem should be approached. If you think a telephone survey or focus group is the way to go, say so, and explain why. If appropriate, discuss how similar research was conducted for you in the past. Note the good and bad aspects of past studies done for you. The goal is to provide enough information so a potential researcher can candidly address your problem.

Solicited firms should be asked to provide a detailed technical plan that outlines each step in the research process. Tell them you want data analysis and sampling plans. Ask them to justify each element of their technical plan. Have them provide a calendar, Gantt chart, or PERT flow diagram of activities in the research process. This will give you a visual picture of the activities, their relationship to each other, and the time line. Of course, request that they submit an itemized budget. No budget, no deal.

Ask for their managerial plan. Request a brief history of the company and its mission, a client list, and a summary of past studies they have conducted that are similar to what you are asking for. Ask who will be responsible for which operations. Have them include an organizational chart and biographical sketches of key personnel, plus anything else they deem germane. Tell them when the proposal is due. Allow one to two weeks for responses. Provide your name and telephone number so they can ask you pertinent questions that were omitted from the rfp.

Once all proposals are in, filter out bad ones. Call these firms or write them a personal letter and reject them. In other words, do not leave them hanging. You owe them basic consideration, but not detailed reasons. Say their proposals did not meet your needs. After the bad ones are filtered out, attend to the good ones.

What constitutes a winning proposal? Several things. Budget and time are two major considerations, but not the only deciding factors. Past studies, resources, and company reputation have value, but are not prime determinants. The technical plan is the most important element of the proposal. What they plan to do and why is what you should focus on. Based on all factors, narrow the competition down to two or three firms. Interview them on their premises (if feasible) and ask key people detailed questions on method.

Assuming your top three choices are all squared away, how do you make that final selection? If you like one firm's approach but cannot afford their price, ask how they can compromise. If they want your business, and they do, they will figure out a way. Another alternative is to go to an independent research consultant, such as a marketing research professor, and ask for a second opinion. Pay that person to help you make that final choice. You will save a lot of money in the long run. After consultation with an outside expert and colleagues within your company, select the outside firm. Your next step is to meet with the research agency and work out the details. One word on morality: it is unethical to review an agency's solicited technical plan and then execute their plan yourself or through another agency. If you want to use an agency's plan but not them, purchase the plan from them. That way you get the best plan and they get money and credit for their ideas.

WHAT TO DO AFTER YOU DECIDE WHO WILL DO THE RESEARCH

Whether you, your staff, the research department, an outside firm, or some combination of the above conducts the research, you should remain in control of the project. By control, I do not mean that you dictate every move, but rather you give and receive input at each stage of the research process. You will want to monitor and evaluate each step to ensure accuracy and cost-effectiveness. If you use an outside agency, insist that you be apprised of all major decisions, changes, and glitches so you can respond. Keep in close contact with those who conduct your research.

The remaining chapters focus on cost-effective ways of conducting different types of research. Only the most tried and true or most promising methods are discussed. Ways of minimizing error and improving validity are presented, along with rules of thumb for doing or supervising the study. Chapter two centers on secondary research, the most inexpensive and quickest way to obtain information. Chapter three covers surveying, the most popular research method, and chapter four highlights depth interviews and focus groups, techniques rapidly growing in popularity and applications. Chapter five deals with ethnographic, or naturalistic research, and structured observation. Behavior, rather than beliefs and attitudes, provides the focus for this chapter. Experimental research, potentially the most cost-effective way to get the best information, is the topic of Chapter six. I provide the most direct and inexpensive ways to process and analyze data in Chapter seven. The final chapter details how information must be presented for it to achieve its purpose. These chapters will help you answer the multitude of research questions posed at the opening of Chapter one.

2

Using Secondary Information

Part of Chapter one focused on who should conduct a given research project; selecting proper people saves money and energy. I argued that marketing research is necessary regardless of company size and market share. I argued against using complex decision tree methods to cost out research value. Reasons? Bayesian models take a long time to figure and thus cost time and money. Also, all input data must be correct or projections will be wrong. So, an armchair cost analyst should look for the least expensive ways to get information. The first place to search is through historical records, secondary data, which is available information already collected for another purpose. Those selected to gather information should check out all secondary sources first. Maybe you will get the information you seek at nominal cost. This is ideal.

In this chapter I describe secondary information, its pros and cons, and how to best use it. In-house, outside, computerized, and written secondary sources are examined. I provide tips regarding cost-effective use of secondary and syndicated data.

PROS AND CONS OF SECONDARY DATA

Why use secondary information? It is cheap, often quick and easy to obtain, and sometimes adequate and relevant. Another primary reason to use secondary data is that occasionally the scope and depth of the research are much greater than you could afford or have the expertise to do. That is, secondary research findings can be cheaper, more accurate, and more comprehensive than primary research findings. Every marketing manager should routinely check out available secondary research to spot future trends, threats, or opportunities. This should be part of your job.

Before we get too carried away with the benefits of secondary research, we should state the cons. First, although secondary data may be available, it may not be relevant enough to fit your specific needs. And, unless it is data you have gathered, it may not be reliable and valid. That is, there may be errors in the data that you cannot assess or detect because you did not conduct or control the research. Further, even though it is quick to get, it may not be timely. Old information is like yesterday's paper; who needs it?

To capitalize on the pros and minimize the cons, here are a few general tips to use when evaluating secondary information. Be thorough. Investigate recent, major secondary sources within and outside your company. Check your professional associations, governmental monitoring agencies, and trade journals and other publications for secondary research possibilities. Keep industry indices on hand. According to Barker (1982: 32), for $400 you can purchase all the the indices you need to obtain sales information and marketing data on your industry. This is cheap.

When reviewing secondary information, especially that obtained from sources outside your company, there are several factors to consider. First, check the source. Who was the person or organization responsible? Is this person's track record good? A cautionary note: even if an organization or individual has a good reputation, that does not automatically make their work credible. Anyone can err or fudge. Also, just because an agency has no history does not make their work suspect. Another tip: always use the primary data source. Never rely on someone else's interpretation of original research. If you do, you will find yourself that much further away from pertinent details that may affect that study's true value to you.

When reviewing a piece of research, ascertain the author's purpose, methods, sample, data analysis procedures, and interpretation. Find out what they omitted, not just what they committed. What you do not know can hurt you as much or more as what you do know about the data. To help you determine the value of secondary research, two works are recommended. The first is a chapter in a book that tells the reader how to understand a research article (see Huck, Cormier, & Bounds 1974: 3–16). The second source is a book on secondary research by Stewart (1984). You can also refer to standard marketing research texts in your company marketing library.

IN-HOUSE SOURCES

Once you feel you can adequately determine the value of secondary research, you must then conduct the search. The first place to look is in-house. This is the most accessible, probably the most pertinent, and likely the most verifiable secondary data you will find. You have three in-house sources: files and records, the company library, and your marketing information system (MIS) database. Let's discuss each.

Files and Records

It pays to keep cross-referenced files on hand that cover all aspects of marketing and sales. These records aid in forecasting and auditing—and cover your flanks. What should be included in your files? Everything you can imagine about the marketing domain in your company, plus warrantee questionnaires, data from production and operations, and anything else you can think of. A complete manual filing system is the barest essential of internal secondary data.

Company Library

Your company library should contain all those indices you can purchase for $400, plus all trade journals and related publications. Additionally, your marketing library should contain general and special marketing and research journals and books. Many of the articles and books mentioned or discussed here are good candidates for your research library. For a few hundred dollars, you can obtain classic works that will enhance your market research knowledge base. All past primary and syndicated research should also be filed in your company library. In short, anything relevant to your industry should reside in your company library. A library takes up little space and is essential.

Company Databases

Your company uses computers, right? You have access to a personal computer. Do you use it to help solve marketing problems? You should. By the 1990s, I predict that most marketers in medium-size and large companies will use their PCs to store data about their sales history, the competition, sales leads, and consumer demographics—and even psychographics (lifestyle data, opinions, interests, activities). Marketing managers will use these databases with inexpensive software to forecast and simulate market decisions. However, there is no need to wait years for this opportunity. The software and technology are available now at reasonable prices. Your best bet is to beat the herd. Make your computer work for you. Here is what you should do.

First, use your computer to establish in-house databases. Start putting together bibliographic databases that contain citations to relevant publications; directory databases that contain names of clients, vendors, organizations; text databases that house entire source documents; and numeric databases that contain survey results, sales history, purchased data sets, and anything else that contains numbers subject to statistical analysis. Make or buy software that will make this possible. Seek out a MIS consultant to help you set up your system, purchase or construct software, get hardware such as modems and plotters, and link into a telecommunications network.

Be judicious when deciding what materials and equipment you need. Make your money go far, and remember, things are changing fast in the information industry. In a few years, PCs will be able to handle huge datasets that only mainframes can deal with presently. You should not wait, but start computerizing your files and library now. The good news is that all this modern stuff occupies very little space and gives you inexpensive and instant access to your company's data and information from all over the world.

OUTSIDE SOURCES

In addition to computerizing your internal records, you should also check out electronic databases that can contribute to your decisions—instantly.

Information Retrieval Services

Who offers the most comprehensive database in the world? The U.S. Census Bureau. You can access its many databases. Just order the current *Census Catalog and Guide* from the Government Printing Office (Washington, DC) to see what is available. The cost is nominal ($21 in 1987). The Census Bureau, in addition to its United States database, also offers a world database in diskette form. Its International Data Base (IDB) provides information on 203 countries, including methods used and qualifications. Key demographics and statistics for each country are provided, again for a nominal cost. This is an example of one service of the Bureau of the Census. Publications such as *Business America* and *Population Bulletin* provide information and updates on what the Bureau can provide. Without a doubt, census data is the most valuable and economical tool around. Learn how to use the census. Some companies specialize in providing census data in easy-to-use form for marketers (examples include CACI, and National Decision Systems). You may wish to use their services.

There are many other useful databases that can be accessed electronically or purchased directly or through vendors. Unless you really know what you are doing, I advise you to seek out a quality vendor. Check their prices and services, and use vendors that give you the best deal. There are currently hundreds of computerized information vendors. I suggest you search the literature to find vendors who can assist you with your specific needs. A few of the larger vendors include Compuserve, Dialog Information Service, News Net, Telmar Media Systems, and Mead Data Central.

Some of these services are reviewed in publications such as *Business Marketing, Marketing News, Advertising Age, Sales and Marketing Management,* and *Marketing.* For example, one vendor, Mead Data Central, offers electronic access to full-text periodicals and databases. *Marketing News* showcases Mead Data in an article (Bockelman 1986: 24). Many vendors also advertise in these publications. Investigate them.

When choosing databases, you should consider several factors: the type and form of information desired, the data bases best able to provide that information, and who offers the database or access to it. Learn how to search through databases so information can be found efficiently. Public and university libraries may contain directories and guides to databases, as well as free on-line access to a database of books in print. The American Library Association sells a database sourcebook, as does a Santa Monica firm, Cuadra Associates, among others. Obtain these.

When purchasing on-line industry studies, McCarrier (1987: 5) advises that you ask these questions before deciding. Does price reflect detail and accuracy you expect? Are scope and methods mentioned in the table of contents? Once you purchase the study, he recommends that you ask several questions. Do tables and graphs contain complete citations? If a survey, is response rate indicated? Are numbers represented in percentages, and if so, are the original sample numbers included? Does the study include contacts at organizations listed? How are forecasts made? These and similar questions should always be foremost in your mind when obtaining and reviewing on-line studies. Apply the caveats and tips for evaluating secondary information provided earlier in this chapter. You will find that electronically accessing government and private databases can be cost-effective, if done judiciously.

Print Media

In addition to or in lieu of on-line information, you should use public and university libraries for information in print. Although the library may be slower in providing information than computer and telecommunications equipment, you are assured of getting the original source, not an abstract. In the case of reviewing original research from journals, you get the complete article and the latest published studies. And the information is free. All you have to do is go get it.

Surprisingly, many college graduates are inept at maximizing the services of a library. My advice is to tour the library and become familiar with it. Most libraries offer guided tours. Most librarians can answer all your questions and help you find what you need.

Here is an efficient way to glean all the information a library has on a given subject. First, go to the abstracts and indexes section of the library and find the index that covers the general subject area. Look up key words under the specific section and photocopy all pages with promising sources. Go to the periodicals shelves and locate all promising articles. Promising means recent or benchmark studies. Read the article abstracts and check the list of references. From the reference list, you may find other articles to copy or journals to peruse. If the piece looks good, photocopy it and write the bibliographic citation on the first page. Store all photocopied articles in a file. Next, go to the "recent issues" section of the library and search through the past four issues of all journals that have potential. Again, look for promising articles.

Another good way to use the library is to access books and articles electronically. Many university libraries feature InfoTrac or some other electronic search system. After you provide the computer with key words (such as subject), a printout will list all sources on file under your requested heading. You simply go get them and follow the procedure described above. In a few hours you can be the proud owner of a wealth of information on a given subject. Then, sort through it all and decide which studies have merit using the criteria for evaluating secondary information provided earlier. Note this: access terminals are convenient but electronic bibliographies are incomplete and should not be considered the only way to access print media. In a few years, electronic bibliographies will compete with printed indices. In the meantime, always check electronic and printed indices to get the whole picture.

What do you do when you have a lot of evidence gathered on a single topic? You can eyeball the literature and make subjective judgments. This is often done. But, what if the data are results of several experiments on a single subject, say the toxicity of saccharin? Different experiments come up with different results. Which is correct? Do you believe the conclusions of one researcher over another? Do you judge by sample size? Assuming the research was conducted properly (review the methods section), all you need do is examine the results across the studies of interest. By results I refer to effect size and its accuracy (e.g., confidence interval). By applying a series of algebraic equations, an overall effect size and accuracy can be obtained. For an excellent treatise on this subject, read Rosenthal's (1984) *Meta-analytic Procedures for Social Research* (also read Glass, McGaw, & Smith 1981). Your company statistician or a university statistician can assist you with meta-analysis questions. Meta-analysis is another cost-effective method to apply to experimental results available as secondary data. Check it out.

SYNDICATED RESEARCH

Let us now discuss the merits of syndicated research, which is data collected in a systematic and regular basis by a research supplier for a particular industry. Anyone in the industry can purchase the results. The main advantage of syndicated research is lower cost. To conduct a similar study to compare yourself against industry competitors would be prohibitively expensive, so syndicated research is definitely cost-effective, in most instances.

Syndicated research lies in the gray area between secondary and primary research. You buy the primary research from a syndicated research supplier, but the study is commissioned for a specific purpose, which may not be your exact purpose. Most syndicated sources can be classified into three areas: diary panels, store audits, and electronic scanner data. Syndicated research is used most in consumer package goods industries.

There are weaknesses and strengths to each method noted above. Diary purchase panels and media panels require people to report on their product use, and people do not always report accurately, for various reasons. Nielsen, Arbitron, and other companies have recently introduced electronic recording devices to augment and/or replace the traditional media panel diaries, but these devices are also fraught with reliability and validity problems.

Warehouse and retail auditing techniques systematically check to see how much a product has been withdrawn from a warehouse or sold at the retail level. These tried and true methods now face stiff competition from electronic scanner services. Due to universal product codes

(UPCs) and electronic optical checkout devices being widely used, direct and timely observation of purchase behavior is now available in many places in the United States. Soon, electronic scanner methods will be commonplace everywhere. In the meantime, scanner data may not be representative because smaller markets have yet to offer the service. The point is to show that syndicated research is widely used but not perfect. Syndicated research alone usually will not suffice for most companies. Here is an example.

Suppose you owned a string of radio stations in large cities across the country. Say your stations offered a specialty type of format such as jazz. Your listening share for each station may not be very high. Thus it may not pay to rely on Arbitron to tell you that your station in San Francisco captures almost one percent of the total listening sample. You may need to entice advertisers with alternative information, such as results from a custom survey in each city that breaks down the demographics and psychographics of your listeners and reports what activities they participate in and what products and services they buy. These custom surveys could be used along with or in lieu of Arbitron ratings. This would be a cost-effective way to obtain useful information that could bring in revenue to your stations.

This is but one example. Hopefully, it will serve to illustrate the point that syndicated research has its place in a company's research portfolio, but syndicated sources are far from perfect and may not offer the best answer in your situation. A wise marketing manager will weigh the costs and benefits of syndicated versus secondary and custom primary research. In chapter three we examine the most popular primary research method—the survey.

3

Surveying

If you want to know what people *think* the best way to find out is to ask them. There are two primary ways to ask people what they think: conduct depth interviews with individuals or groups (the subject of chapter four), or survey a representative sample of a population using a questionnaire. Here we discuss the latter. For surveying to be accurate, relevant, timely—and cost-effective, you must consider several factors. Four of the steps in the research process need to be dealt with. Step four concerns developing data collection forms and methods. Step five centers on laying out your data analysis plan to fit your questionnaire and information needs. Step six involves selection of a sample. Finally, step seven details the actual collection of the data from respondents.

In this chapter we describe surveying and when to use it. We examine question types, number formats, attitude scales, and question sequencing—and tying these in to your data analysis plan. We discuss how to ask sensitive questions. We tackle the complex subject of sample selection and size. We debate the merits of the three ways of collecting survey data and focus on ways of minimizing nonsampling error. Finally, we comment on field procedures used when collecting survey data.

WHEN TO SURVEY

Survey when you want a description of a target population's beliefs about themselves, your products, the future, anything. Survey when you want to find out how much consumers know, how they feel about something, what behavior they did in the past, and what they intend to do in the future. Use surveying when you want a description of consumers and their opinions, interests, and activities. These data are what marketing managers want to know most. This is probably why the survey is the most used research method. Surveying is also the method of choice for tracking, positioning, and segmentation studies—and is even used in experimentation.

Surveying is relatively straightforward, but is more of an art than a science. Often you will see many ways to design a questionnaire, select a sample, or collect data. Each alternative has merit. The researcher's job is to decide which alternative in each instance will best meet the research objective at the lowest cost. Here, I provide a few tips to help you make choices more clearly.

Before we list rules of thumb in surveying, there are a few overriding concerns that must always be addressed when conducting surveys. First, as mentioned earlier, make sure that you choose competent people to design the questionnaire, select the sampling procedure and size, determine data collection method, and conduct the survey and data analysis. Choosing the wrong people can mean your company pays an outrageous price and receives a report full of tables with no interpretation or recommendations, or worse, a slick report that omits key details in method.

Before you begin data collection, make sure you have precisely defined the population of interest and have an adequate sample list to draw a representative sample. Try to ensure that selected respondents are able and willing to complete the survey. Figure out how you will deal with nonresponse due to refusals. Speaking of refusals, here are a few other things to consider before you begin surveying.

Be ethical. Do not abuse respondent rights. Keep promises made to respondents. Do not cause stress to the interviewee. Never sell under guise. Do not insist on interviewing a person who refuses. The list goes on. The point is, you need respondents to answer candidly. Thus you must be considerate. Many people are tired of being abused as guinea pigs so someone can profit. Surveying is expensive. If people refuse to answer, or distort answers, you spend a lot of money for nothing. This is a growing problem in survey research, so think about it. Let us now look at essential areas of surveying, starting with measurement instruments.

QUESTIONNAIRE CONSTRUCTION

Constructing questionnaires is an art, and it seems that a professional marketing researcher would be artistic, but this is not always so. Every day I see shoddy, ineffectual, unethical questionnaires. The worst I have seen since the early 1970s was the Sierra Club's Environmental Priorities Survey. This research was a marketing scam for their membership drive. I admire the club's stated ideals, but detest their selling-under-guise-of-research ploy. As I stated earlier, researchers must be ethical.

Format

Rather than discuss bad questionnaires, let us deal with constructing good questionnaires. First, let us start with the preamble, or the introduction to the questionnaire. Whether your questionnaire is mailed or read by an interviewer, an introduction is needed. Start by identifying the interviewer. Then briefly state the purpose of the survey. If stating the purpose would bias respondents' answers, construct a cover story that shields the true nature of the survey but does not cause psychological harm to respondents. Be ethical. If possible, debrief respondents as to the true purpose of the survey after you finish. After the cover story, state how long it will take the person to complete the survey. State if responses are to be confidential and/or anonymous.

Next, qualify the respondent. If interviewing by telephone, ask for whoever you need to speak to. If surveying by mail, write that only the designated respondent should complete the questionnaire. Your first couple of questions should be filter questions to ensure that you have the correct respondent. Ask a question relating directly to the purpose that tests the respondent's awareness or interest. In short, make sure the respondent is qualified to answer questions.

Next, get to the main body of questions. Start right off asking questions relating to the stated purpose. This is necessary to reduce the respondent's suspicion about the authenticity of your request for information. The sequence of questions should be specific to general, or the converse. Questions that share the same metric should be asked in a sequence. Questions on the same topic should be placed together. When asking questions, start with those that are easy to answer, then move to more complex items. When asking for opinions, first gauge the respondents' awareness and knowledge level, then ask for unaided beliefs about attributes of the topic. Then supply more information and ask for beliefs. Give cues if necessary. Ask attitude, or "how do you feel about . . ." questions next. Probe to find out why they feel the way they do.

Finish the sequence with questions regarding intentions for their future behavior. Ask only necessary questions. Do not waste the respondent's time by asking questions that may benefit your company in a few years. After the respondent is warmed up, ask sensitive questions. Finish the survey with demographic questions. End with "Thank you."

It is permissable to use a contingency approach to questions, where some questions are skipped if a certain response is given (branching). Make sure the "skipping" instructions are clear so the interviewer or respondent does not get confused.

Here are some final words regarding format. Make your questionnaire appear crisp, clear, uncluttered, and professional. Put all the response categories in the same place. The best place is on the right-hand margin, so the data entry operator can easily read responses and the person responding does not have to search for the place to put the answer.

Developing Questions

Your first decision in developing questions is whether to make the questions open-end or closed-end. Open-end is often used in depth interviewing to get respondents to open up in their own words. These questions have no response categories and numbers are not used. Open-end questions are used in surveys during pilot testing to help develop closed-end categories and in finished surveys to allow respondents to make "additional remarks." Otherwise, open-end questions should not be used in surveying because responses are vague, rambling, difficult to interpret, and almost impossible to compare with other responses in a meaningful way. And, open-end questions are three to five times as costly to analyze as closed-end questions, according to Pope (1981: 6). The rule of thumb is: Use closed-end questions, that is, questions that feature numbers for responses.

Before making specific types of closed-end questions, make sure your questions adequately address the information needs and research objectives set by the decision makers. Then construct your questions, focusing on several aspects.

First, focus on phrasing. Make sure you use shared language, and that questions are clear and simple. Avoid writing questions that contain emotionally "loaded" words that excite respondents' feelings and thus bias their responses. Do not lead respondents into answering in a prescribed manner. Make sure a question asks only one question. Avoid asking people to estimate or guess. Questions should be worded in such a way that respondents can answer concisely and candidly.

Next, focus on number formats. Decide the type of data you wish to analyze later with statistics. For each question, determine which type of numerical answer best fits your needs: category (nominal), where numbers merely represent an object or idea (e.g., 1 = yes, 2 = no); ranking (ordinal), where numbers show a greater than/less than relationship (e.g., "Rank these items in order of preference"); rating (interval), where numbers appear to be in equal intervals to measure an attribute of an object (e.g., "Rate this item on a scale from 1 to 7, with 1 being 'ugly' and 7 being 'beautiful'"); and score (ratio), where numbers possess an absolute zero and magnitude between numbers can be compared (e.g., market share).

It is important always to consciously choose your number format because the format determines the complexity and amount of information that a number can provide. A nominal number is simplest to understand and easiest to deal with statistically. However, categories do not provide much information. They state only whether or not a person or object is included or excluded from a category. Ordinal questions are used in marketing research to ask respondents to gauge similarity or preference among brands. This type of data is good but does not tell you the degree of preference. Interval scales are used to obtain means that can be used with powerful statistics such as analysis of variance and regression. Interval data are sensitive, but not absolute in magnitude. Some statisticians argue that many interval scales are actually ordinal and only express greater than/less than relationships. Without question, ratio numbers provide the most powerful data.

Ratio data can be broken down to nominal data and analyzed as such, but the converse is not true. For example, we could convert a score on a test to a pass/fail category, but we could not convert a "pass" to a score. Here is another example. If you were conducting a beer consumption survey, you could ask, "Have you drunk beer during the past week?" Or, you could ask, "How many beers have you drunk during the past week?" The second question, a ratio question, is more sensitive. It provides more quantitative data. As a general rule, quantitative is better than qualitative. As a rule, ratio beats interval, interval beats ordinal, ordinal beats nominal. The nature of your information needs will decide which numerical format will serve you best. As mentioned earlier, because of data analysis considerations, you must choose which number types work best with each question.

Scales

To ascertain people's beliefs, attitudes, and intentions, many scales have been developed and used over the years. Some are nominal yes/no categories; others are more complex ordinal and interval scales. If you need to rank or order variables, ordinal scales would be appropriate.

When we get to "equally appearing" interval scales, the trouble—and the fun—begins.

One of the assumptions of interval data is equality of distance. That is, we assume that respondents perceive differences between words (such as "strongly agree" and "agree") to be equally spaced numerically. So we assign numbers to words. "Strongly agree" would equal 5, "agree" would equal 4, "neither agree or disagree" would equal 3, "disagree" would equal 2, and "strongly disagree" would equal 1. We want to use a sensitive interval scale as input for powerful statistics. It is important to link numerical values with their verbal descriptions, or else it is difficult to claim that respondents viewed responses as equally spaced.

Notice that in the above example of an interval scale (Likert scale), there was a "neutral" response. Most attitude scales contain this neutral response to account for a respondent's neutrality on a subject. This is common. Occasionally, you may wish to construct a "forced" scale with the neutral response eliminated. This would be done if you knew that respondents were not neutral on the topic, but would be likely to choose the neutral response to avoid commitment on the issues. If you think some respondents may have no opinion about the subject of the question, then make available a "No opinion" category outside the response format.

Here are some common interval rating scales. The semantic differential is a seven-point bipolar adjective scale used to rate products on several dimensions, such as "light-heavy" or "good-bad." Average consumer profiles can be graphed from this data. A Stapel scale is similar to the semantic differential, but uses a ten-point unipolar scale. Average consumer profiles on attributes can also be constructed with a Stapel scale.

The Likert scale (agree/disagree) noted earlier is used often. A respondent is given a series of statements about an object and is asked to agree or disagree with the statements using the scale. The scale is usually five-point, but occasionally a three-point or seven-point version is used. Research conducted by Soares and Ray (1986) showed that a three-point Likert scale gave equivalent results to a five-point scale—even over the telephone.

Other interval scales used include continuous rating and itemized rating scales. Continuous rating scales ask the respondent to assign a rating by marking a position on a line anchored with responses such as "favorable-unfavorable." Itemized rating scales are similar, but the line is broken into equally appearing intervals. Each small line contains a descriptive response and a corresponding number. A typical itemized response question would list an item and ask the rater to mark whether it was "extremely bad," "rather bad" "neither bad nor good," "rather good," and "extremely good."

There are many scales. You should refer to a general marketing research text or a specialized guide to help you decide which rating scale would best fit your needs. If you need to ask complex sequences of attitude and opinion scales, your best bet is to secure a research firm or individual who specializes in attitude scales. There are issues of validity and reliability that need to be accounted for when developing scales. Your best bet is to keep your questionnaire simple. Exclude rating scales unless you absolutely must use them. Opt for narrower response categories rather than wide ones, especially if you are conducting your survey with telephone interviewers. The more responses you include, the more awkward your data analysis becomes. So, do not include capricious categories or use a nine-point scale on a whim. However, if your research needs demand several categories or a more sensitive scale, then do it.

Asking Difficult Questions

Asking people certain questions can be difficult. Certain questions are too personal, and many people do not want to answer. And if they do, they may distort the truth, or lie outright. Some of these difficult questions are demographic items such as age, political party, or income. Other difficult questions may relate directly to the primary topic of your survey. Examples of these questions might include: "Have you cheated on your spouse?" "Have you taken illegal drugs?" "Have you been audited by the IRS?" People may give you a socially desirable answer or refuse to continue with the survey. All you want is candor. What should you do?

First, do not ask sensitive questions unless you must. Second, put them near the end of the questionnaire, after the respondent is warmed up. Third, ask the question in a nonthreatening manner. For example, during a telephone interview, you would ask the income question this way: "Please stop me when I reach your combined family income level—0 to 10,000 dollars, 10 to 20,000, 20 to 30, 30 to 40, 40 to 50, more?" Another way to ask a sensitive question is to precede it with an explanation. "Every year, thousands of Americans are audited by the IRS. Have you?" If the survey contains many of these questions, broach the subject in the preamble, so the respondent is fully aware of the situation. If you are conducting a personal interview, devise a way that the respondent can answer the question anonymously, without the interviewer knowing the response. You could have the respondent place the answer into a box. Alternatively, you could show the respondent a card with numbers below responses. Ask the respondent to "just state the number, not the words." This makes it easier for respondents to answer truthfully.

Mail surveys work best when asking sensitive questions, because the respondent does not have to face the interviewer. This only works when there are no identifying numbers, codes, or questions on the questionnaire. Also, you must assure the respondent anonymity and confidentiality. And instruct the respondent to follow the question sequence without skipping ahead.

One thing you do not want to do is ask a question in such a way that you are unsure if the answer is the respondent's true response. Do not ask questions such as "What would the 'average' person do in this situation?" Respondents may tell you what the average person would do, and not what they would do. Stay away from projective techniques where respondents complete sentences or describe what a picture means. Interpreting such data is highly subjective, requires a clinical or industrial psychologist, and is usually expensive. There are few instances where a projective technique would overshadow direct questioning.

Also, avoid randomized response techniques (see Campbell and Joiner 1973) where the respondent is asked two yes or no questions. One question is sensitive; the other is not. A coin toss determines the question to be answered. A statistician later figures the probability of the sensitive question being answered. This technique is cumbersome for the interviewer and respondent, works only for yes or no questions, and relies on random chance with its associated random error. It may or may not measure the true response.

There are other issues in questionnaire design and question wording not covered here. I advise you to critique a number of questionnaires, and refer to books and articles that will help you with this fine art. One good reference book is Labaw's (1980) *Advanced Questionnaire Design.* Also see Payne's (1951) *The Art of Asking Questions.* Finally, you should consider attending a questionnaire design workshop sponsored by the American Marketing Association or other reputable organization.

SAMPLING

A major cost to consider when designing surveys is sampling procedure and sample size. Some sampling procedures are easier and thus cost-efficient. A smaller sample size means lower cost. But there are many trade-offs and considerations. Let's discuss these, beginning with sampling procedures.

Sampling Procedures

There are two major classes of sampling procedures, probability and nonprobability methods. In probability methods, each subject has a known probability of being selected to a study. In probability sampling, sampling error is generated and statistical efficiency can be measured. Probability procedures include simple random sampling and its cousin, systematic random sampling; stratified sampling; cluster and area sampling; and multistage sampling, which combines some of the above methods. In probability sampling, a statistician can estimate an efficient sample size based on allowable error, confidence level desired, and expected variation. These are discussed later.

Nonprobability sampling makes none of these assumptions. Sampling error cannot be computed. There is no known probability of a subject being included in a sample. Thus a nonprobability sample is less likely than a probability sample to truly represent its population. At the least, you have no sure way of knowing how representative a nonprobability sample is. There are several types of nonprobability techniques: convenience sampling, quota sampling, judgment or expert opinion sampling, and unique sampling methods such as snowball. Let's examine nonprobability methods.

Nonprobability Methods. Convenience sampling, where subjects are selected based on whoever is "conveniently" available (not to be confused with "random" sampling, the probability method), is easy and used extensively in marketing research studies. This is a good method for exploratory research, or when any person will do, or when data are needed quickly and convenient subjects are readily available. If your research need is one of these, choose a convenience sample.

Quota sampling is simply convenience sampling coupled with a need to obtain proportions of people on a given variable. For example, if you were conducting a mall intercept study and needed a proportionate amount of people based on their ethnicity, you could instruct interviewers to choose 50 percent whites, 20 percent blacks, 15 percent Hispanics, and 15 percent Asians, based on the ethnic breakdown of the neighborhood. Again, this method is used extensively, and is likely to be more representative than convenience sampling. It is also considered an inexpensive way to select subjects who are readily available. You should choose quota sampling if your needs are the same as for a convenience sample and you have relevant demographic variables from which to draw quotas.

Judgment sampling involves an "expert" determining who should be included in a survey based upon "judgment." This method is straightforward and useful when the population of interest is small, difficult to reach, and a trusted expert is available. This method is used moderately in practice and is inexpensive, due largely to small samples obtained.

Sometimes a unique problem may require a census or special sampling technique, such as snowball sampling. If the population is small, easy to reach, and widely varied, a census or partial census of that population may be your best bet. However, if your population is small and difficult to reach, such as marijuana growers, you may need to use a snowball sample. Snowball sampling is borrowed from the sales profession, where customers are asked to provide names of other prospects. In snowball sampling, a respondent is asked to name all other people who share the same attribute of interest. These people are contacted, surveyed, and asked to provide more names. The snowball sampling method is straightforward, cost-effective, and a good way to construct a sampling frame for future study.

The good news is that nonprobability sampling methods are easy and relatively inexpensive. The bad news is that these techniques may not represent the population of interest—and you would have no way of knowing. And, is not representativeness the point of sampling? What good is a research study with responses that may or may not represent your consumers' true beliefs, attitudes, intentions, and behaviors? There is one more point to consider. Many statistical tests are based on probability, and probability is not computable with nonprobability samples. So, be alert when choosing and using nonprobability samples. They may be more expensive than you bargained for.

Probability Methods. I want to discuss and advocate simple random sampling, the best sampling procedure—and a probability method not used enough in marketing research. In simple random sampling (SRS), every population element has an equal chance of being included in the sample. Elements from a population list are assigned numbers and drawn randomly from a hat, random numbers table, roulette wheel, or computer random number generator subroutine. This is a fairly easy procedure and should be used when respondents are homogeneous (very similar) on key variables, or variability estimates are not available, or you do not trust your variability estimates, or it is too difficult to sample respondents proportionately on a key variable. As you can see, researchers often face these situations. Amazingly, they still opt for other sampling methods in the vain hope that they are saving money and/or time. If subjects are easy to reach and per interview field costs are relatively low, SRS should often be the method of choice.

There is another good reason for using SRS. It is not too difficult to compute sample size with SRS, whereas more complex techniques, such as stratified sampling, necessitate consulting with a sampling statistician who may not be familiar with the requirements of your study. The bad news with SRS is that sometimes a larger sample is needed to ensure that representativeness is achieved. This can cost more.

Systematic sampling is used moderately in marketing research. Theoretically, respondents have an equal chance of being selected, just as in SRS. Here, the researcher obtains an adequate population list that exhibits no systematic regularities and, after a random start, chooses every ith unit where $i = n/N$, with n being the sample size and N the population list size. This method is quicker than SRS and requires no numbering of elements. Systematic sampling may save money and is a useful variant of SRS.

Stratified sampling is used moderately in marketing research but is often touted as the cat's meow in marketing research texts. Basically, in stratified sampling, SRS is conducted proportionately (or disproportionately if desired) within strata (levels). Ideally, statistical efficiency is high with stratified sampling, assuming stratification variables work. If they do not, you are left with a mess. Your survey is done, but you sampled based on proportions that were wrong, thus your efficient sample is no longer large enough. A SRS would prevent this. A stratified sampling method based on location is called an area sample. This method is used extensively in personal interviewing situations when tract dwellings are the unit of study. The area sample is a hybrid between stratified sampling and cluster sampling.

Cluster sampling is another probability method. It works like this. The population is divided into representative groups called clusters. Clusters are randomly sampled and all the people in the cluster are surveyed. This is convenient and cost-effective on a per interview basis, but may be expensive from a sample size perspective since it often requires more people to adequately represent the population.

Sometimes a two-stage cluster sample is used. Here clusters are randomly sampled and people within the cluster are also randomly sampled. If several samplings are done to reach selected respondents, it is called multistage sampling. This is complex and requires the services of a sampling statistician.

Tips for Choosing a Sampling Method

When choosing a sampling method, consider these thoughts. You want to reduce nonsampling errors, so choose a method that will help you do this. If representativeness and accuracy are not that important, but speed or low cost are essential, your best bet is to go with a nonprobability method such as judgment or quota. You will not require a sampling statistician to help you, and will save money and time. If representativeness and measuring sampling error are important, choose a probability method that will best meet your research objectives and save your company money. Of all the methods available, I recommend SRS in general. It is the one probability method that will not fail you. It is relatively easy to select a sample size (read the proceding section) and to obtain the samples. Most statistics and canned software packages are set up for use with random samples. And you stay close to your data and respondents. You do not have to rely on a lot of assumptions about respondent variability that may or may not hold water.

The method of choosing a sample is very important in any research situation. If unsure, consult with a sampling statistician. Read your marketing research texts, and obtain sampling methods references and manuals for your company library (see Cochran 1977; Kalton 1983; Kish 1965; Sudman 1976; Yates 1981). Let us now turn to sample size.

Sample Size

What contributes most to the cost of a survey? Per interview costs—the costs to survey and process each respondent's input. Thus the more people you survey, the more it costs. What you want to do is select the fewest amount of people needed to adequately represent the population of study. All you need are enough people so another researcher could replicate your survey and get equivalent results. You do not need 50,000 respondents, as some magazines brag about in their readership surveys. Oftentimes, 50,000 people who self-select to participate in a survey do not adequately represent the population of interest. Never be tricked by enormous sample sizes. In pure research, as contrasted with applied marketing research, sample sizes are often seemingly small, especially in experimental and clinical research. In some fields, such as speech pathology, some studies use only ten subjects and yet get published. In a recent speech pathology study, a colleague and I approached the outer limits of sample size in that field by using 75 subjects (see Solomon & Soares 1987).

So, how many subjects do you need? Which criteria should you use to determine sample size? This is the area where most decision makers and researchers find trouble. Let's look at two primary criteria relating to sample size— situational priorities and statistical concerns.

Situational factors that affect sample size. Your statistician may calculate an ideal sample size for a project, but your limited budget precludes a large number of people. So, the money allotted for the project is often the determining factor in sample size estimation. You may have to alter your data collection method or sacrifice time or something else to ensure an adequate sample size when constrained by lack of funds. For example, you may have to dump your planned personal interview method in favor of phone interviewing to lower per respondent costs. If you have to sacrifice too much, you might consider abandoning the whole project or increasing the budget.

Another situational factor to consider deals with data analysis. How many groups and subgroups do you wish to analyze and compare with each other? A good rule of thumb is to make sure that you end up with at least 30 people in your smallest group, regardless of the sampling procedure you use. This will allow you to use most statistics with confidence. If you have solid information about a subgroup's variability, you may get by with fewer than 30 respondents. Another rule of thumb regarding sample size that I recommend is 1,000 people per survey, if detailed subgroup data are not needed. If your information needs demand subgroup analysis, then double the sample size to 2,000 respondents. Again, make sure you have at least 30 respondents per subgroup. If you need to perform many subgroup comparisons, then your sample may exceed 3,000.

There are other situational factors that influence sample size. Sackmary (1985: 30) argued that some studies include samples that are larger than needed statistically, and thus more costly, due to decision makers' expectations. He cited examples of excessive sample sizes due to research users' desires to please customers or personnel within the organization, or to ward off criticism from within or from outsite forces. Sackmary recommended that researchers consider the human factor along with budgetary and statistical concerns when determining sample size. I agree. You may need to stress to superiors the benefits (cost-effectiveness and statistical adequacy) of a smaller versus a larger sample.

Statistical aspects of sample size. This is the hard part, even though straightforward mathematical algorithms are available to calculate sample size. Several factors contribute to sample size difficulties. The first difficulty lies in the three basic requirements used to compute optimum sample size: accurate knowledge of population variability, the degree of accuracy desired, and the degree of confidence needed.

Let's start with foreknowledge of population variability. The more variability, the larger sample you need. Obtaining a recent, accurate variability estimate of key population parameters is not always easy. If you rely on U.S. Census figures or extrapolations, these may either be out of date or just estimates. If you refer to a previous study you face the uncertainties presented with secondary research. If you conduct a pilot study to assess variability, your sample will be too small to adequately represent population parameters. I advise that you assume greater variability in the population. So, in the absence of certainty, assume a 50/50 over a 60/40 percentage.

As far as desired accuracy and confidence go, you need merely state your desire. A good rule of thumb for accuracy (precision) is to assume that the true parameter lies three percentage points on either side of an obtained percentage. A good rule of thumb regarding confidence levels (percent of times a sample characteristic lies within specific limits of its population) is to stick with the statistician's standard of 95 percent. So, in a simple random sample with no variability estimate (50/50), 3 percent precision, and 95 percent confidence level, you would need approximately 1,000 respondents. But, there are more difficulties.

Even though there are simple formulas, tables, nomographs, slide calculators, and even computer programs available to calculate sample size, most focus on simple random sampling. Explanations available in most marketing research texts also refer to simple random sampling. If you use stratified or cluster sampling, or multiphase sampling, procedures rapidly become more complex. You may be forced to rely on the services of a sampling statistician. Herein lies the next problem—using statisticians.

Many sampling statisticians are mathematicians by profession. They can calculate sample sizes for complex research designs. Unfortunately, they may not possess enough information about your particular research problem and its accompanying unique circumstances. For example, they may know nothing of the validity of your population variability estimates, assuming you have these. They may not be cognizant of how or why you selected certain variables to study. And, importantly, they may not be aware of your measurement choices or the reasoning behind them. They may not know which statistics you plan to use to analyze your data. What they do not know about your study can adversely affect their calculations.

I recommend using statisticians to determine sample size. To save resources and aid the statistician, be sure to include as much detail as possible, and the reasoning behind your choices. You must inform the statistician of the precise research goals, design and measurement options, sampling procedures, expected response rates, and money available for the study. Then you are likely to obtain the optimum sample size and save money. For more information on sample size considerations, see Kraemer and Thiemann (1987), and Cohen (1977).

COLLECTING SURVEY DATA

There are three ways of collecting survey data: telephone interview, personal interview, and mail survey. Each has its pros and cons. When surveying, the researcher must find the most cost-effective way of collecting data while considering the nature of the information sought, the difficulty in reaching respondents, time constraints, use of resources, and the level of accuracy desired. Let's examine each survey method.

Telephone Interviewing

Overall, telephone interviewing is the best survey method and should be considered first. Here are the reasons why. Telephone interviewing provides accurate data, compared to personal interviewing and mail surveying. You can probe and provide additional clarification, as in personal interviewing, but error associated with nonverbal interaction between interviewer and respondent is greatly reduced by using the telephone.

Complex question formats can be used, even Likert-type attitude scales (see Soares & Ray 1986). If questions asked are salient to the respondent and structured in the proper way, even lengthy surveys can be adequately administered over the telephone. Confidential information can be obtained, if asked for in a diplomatic way.

The response rate for telephone interviewing is fairly good, at least when compared with mail surveying. Assuming your sample can be contacted, the survey is of interest to them, the interviewer is perceived as sincere and ethical, and callbacks are made to reach not-at-homes, you can expect a response rate of about 50 to 75 percent.

Telephone interviews can be very accurate. If interviewers are trained and monitored, and the questionnaire and procedures adequately pilot tested, and responses verified during data entry, you can expect accurate data. With computer-assisted telephone interviewing (CATI), it is possible to ensure even greater accuracy, as the program can signal if a score is out of range and can input data directly into an array. This saves time and reduces human interaction with the data, which lowers error associated with data collection. If you farm out your surveys to a field services company, check to see if they use CATI. If they do, you may save time and money, and get more accurate results. However, it is expensive to purchase CATI software (costs range from $1,000 to $14,000). So, don't buy CATI packages unless your organization plans to telephone interview often.

One of the biggest advantages of telephone interviewing centers on time saved. Telephone interviews can be conducted swiftly, especially with CATI. Sample frames are easy to obtain (telephone directories). By the way, telephone directories serve as excellent and inexpensive sample frames. They are only inappropriate if your study population contains a large number of people who do not list their numbers.

Telephone interviewing is easy to administer. Interviewers can be easily trained. No special college degree is required. Trained interviewers can be monitored at the source, callbacks can be made to respondents, and individual interviewer data can be compared with other interviewers during data analysis to check for consistency.

The primary reason to use telephone interviewing is cost efficiency. Often, telephone interviewing is the least expensive way to obtain quality information. As telephone services improve, direct costs go down, even for long-distance calls. In many cases, telephone data collection is less expensive than mail surveying. Here's why. The response rate of telephone interviewing is twice that of mail. Even though interviewers are not used with mail, the direct cost per completed questionnaire is high. With mail, you pay for the survey, envelopes, and postage. Often you must offer monetary incentives and send follow-up letters and surveys. And to top it off, sometimes you must call to request permission to mail the survey, then call again to remind them to complete it. Mail surveys take weeks to get results, and you end up with half the response rate as you would with the telephone method. In the final analysis, telephone interviewing is usually cheaper than mail interviewing.

The major disadvantage of telephone interviewing lies in visual aids. The respondent cannot see figures, tables, photographs. With major advancements in communications technology being made, many people will have access to videotelephones by the late 1990s and the problem will be solved. In the meantime, you can mail or drop off visual aids to respondents and then call them. If this is not feasible, then another data collection method will have to be used—perhaps the personal interview.

Personal Interviewing

As a general rule, the personal interview is not cost-effective and, therefore, not recommended as a data collection method. It should only be used with small samples in exploratory research where detail and flexibility are paramount. It is the preferred method for focus groups and depth interviews, where open-end, qualitative data will be gathered (the subject of the next chapter). Personal interviewing works best in shopping mall surveys, where respondents are easily accessed.

On the whole, the personal interview should be avoided, unless your research needs dictate its use. Response rates for personal interviews have gone down in area sampling, probably because people do not wish to be hassled by door-to-door canvassers. Personal interviewing is rife with nonsampling error that is difficult to contain or measure. Error associated with the interaction between surveyor and respondent occurs and can influence respondents' answers. To avoid interaction altogether, use a mail survey.

Mail Surveying

Mail surveys work best when operating under a limited budget, or when time is not important, when interaction would contaminate results, when respondents are difficult to reach by telephone, when using a diary, when showing visual aids, when response rate is not an issue, or when asking sensitive questions. Since many people now have access to computers, the mail can be used as a vehicle to interview people via their personal computer, using a questionnaire on a diskette. Simply mail the diskette to the respondent and include a padded envelope. An added bonus of mailed diskette surveys is that the novelty ensures a higher response rate than conventional mail surveys. Of course, the mailed diskette is limited to computer users.

Ordinary mail surveys have weaknesses, also. You are never sure who answered the questionnaire. And there is no way to clarify if a respondent does not understand a question. Finally, many returned questionnaires are not usable because they are incomplete or answers are inconsistent. This reduces the response rate even more.

As you can see, each method has its good and bad points. The telephone method is most preferred; the personal interview is least preferred, at least from a cost-effectiveness standpoint. Sometimes it is best to combine approaches to suit your particular need. Whichever data collection method you use, pay particular attention to field operations.

FIELD OPERATIONS

After spending considerable time and resources on sample selection, questionnaire development, and data collection procedure, you now need to ensure that the actual survey proceeds smoothly. If you are in charge of the project, prepare a Gantt chart (a field time schedule flow diagram) of all activities and their respective time lines. If you have hired an outside firm to conduct the study, ask to see their Gantt chart. This chart is easy to prepare and will help you optimally allocate your budget and resources. Additionally, the chart will provide a tactical plan to monitor and evaluate the study. And, by preparing the chart, you will design the study to avoid or minimize non-sampling errors.

One of the first and most important activities listed on

the chart is pilot testing. It is imperative to pilot test questionnaires and interviewing procedures. Otherwise, error, the enemy, may sabotage your project. Here are some of the nonsampling errors (errors other than differences between sample statistics and population parameters) that judicious pilot testing will uncover.

The first major nonsampling error that pilot sampling will identify is nonresponse error. This occurs when people in a sample cannot be reached or refuse to participate. A pilot survey will provide you with a nonresponse rate estimate. This information can be used to help you replace respondents from your backup sample pool, improve your method of solicitation, or suggest ways to estimate what answers respondents who refused would have given.

Problems in questionnaire design, question sequence and wording, and qualifying respondents can be noted and fixed. Errors that stem from within respondents can be identified, such as inability or unwillingness to answer accurately due to ignorance, forgetfulness, fatigue, anxiety, or social desirability. Additionally, for telephone and personal interviews, pilot testing will pinpoint problem areas within interviewers or the interviewing procedure. For these and other reasons, the pilot test is an integral part of any study and should be included in the research Gantt chart.

Along with the Gantt chart, you may wish to prepare or have prepared a PERT (Program Evaluation Review Technique) or CPM (Critical Path Method) flow diagram to provide an illustration of the processes and activities involved in the project and their relationship to each other. There are inexpensive software packages available that enable you to construct a PERT chart or similar flow diagram with little difficulty.

Yet another design/monitoring device worth considering is a Performance Measures Table (PMT). Here you construct a table with rows representing performance measures (such as eligible respondents, interviews completed, refusals, noncontacts, ineligible respondents, response rate, direct costs per interview) and columns indicating expected versus observed results in each category. This table will help you keep tabs on the project, provide a cost breakdown, and save money on the project and in future related projects. How will it save money? As every operations manager and engineer know, attention to detail in the planning and design stage will save capital later in the project. Plus, should any litigation arise over any element of the study, you will be covered because you did your homework. Avoidable errors will not occur in your research because your plan and test of the plan were sound. So, when conducting a survey—or any research, check and recheck the details before you begin the study, and you will save money and execute lean, accurate research.

4

Depth Interviews and Focus Groups

If people are difficult to reach, or are very knowledgeable in a subject that is important to you, and you want to know what they *think*, the best way to find out is still to ask them. Instead of surveying them, as discussed in the last chapter, conduct depth interviews.

If you are considering introducing a new product, comparing your product with the performance and appeal of a competitor's, or modifying features of an established product, and you want to know what people *think*, the best way to find out is to ask them. In lieu of asking people what they think via a survey, you may wish to gather representative consumers to get together and check out the products in person. This is a focus group.

Depth interviews and focus groups are enjoying a renaissance. Even though standard marketing research texts barely mention these two related methods, their increased popularity shows that many researchers and users of research believe they have merit. These two techniques are described here because they are useful and, most importantly, they are cost-effective. A working knowledge of depth interviewing and focus sessions should be included in all marketing managers' and researchers' quiver of ways to know.

Both methods have many methodological uncertainties that must be dealt with to get your money's worth and ensure that results can be projected to a larger population. So, in this chapter, both techniques are described, pitfalls are noted, and systematic procedures for conducting each type are presented.

DEPTH INTERVIEWING

Depth interviewing is used to obtain rich, exploratory information from a small group of qualified individuals who represent the universe of similar people. These people usually know a lot about a subject of interest. They may be select customers, competitors, industry analysts, technical experts. Oftentimes, these people are difficult to reach or extract information from. Thus researchers must try to get whomever they can to participate.

Depth interviewing is a useful, inexpensive tool to address specific problems facing marketers in the 1990s. Gordon (1987: 22) calls for a "grassroots approach" to pinpointing underlying trends in the marketplace. By "grassroots," Gordon refers to the journalistic practice of querying key sources to tap into the source of events.

Sokolow (1985: 26) recommends depth interviews because they lack the group interaction bias that plagues focus sessions. He adds that marketers want to know "consumers' true needs and desires. . ." He argues that depth interviewing allows respondents to express themselves freely because social desirability fostered within the group is nonexistent, the interviewee receives a great deal of focused attention, and the interviewer can probe and perceive nonverbal feedback easier.

What can depth interviewing do that surveys or focus groups cannot do better? Good question. The depth interview can probe deep into a person's feelings and true motivations. Structured surveys preclude this, and group interaction may inhibit individuals, especially shy people. Another good reason for using depth interviews centers around confidentiality. With proper interviewing techniques, it is more likely that people would reveal sensitive information than they would in a standardized survey situation or in a group. (Knos (1986: 4) adds that busy professionals would rather devote time to a depth interview than to a focus group. These are all good reasons to use the depth interview.

There is one other good reason to utilize the depth interview. It is relatively inexpensive, considering that the interview is personal. Since few people are interviewed (the average is around 30), personal interview time and expense are minimized. Occasionally, it may be appropriate to conduct a depth interview by telephone, and this lowers cost even more.

In depth interviewing, a relatively unstructured, journalistic approach to interviewing is featured. The interviewer poses questions that journalists ask: who, what, where, when, why, how. There are two basic categories of depth interview: nondirective and structured. In nondirective interviewing, the respondent is not restricted. The interviewer is free to pursue the most fruitful avenues of interest. In a structured (focused) interview, the interviewer follows a list of topics and is somewhat more restricted than in the nondirective approach. In both instances, the interview is qualitative. That is, not much quantitative, numerical, statistical, directly comparable data are ordinarily obtained using this approach. Therein lie many of the pitfalls of the depth interview.

Depth Interview Pitfalls

There are problems associated with the depth interview. Some can be surmounted. Here are a few weak points that you must be aware of should you choose this method or should a research firm recommend it. First, due to the qualitative nature of depth interviewing, end users often do not consider results confirmatory, and thus do not base marketing decisions on these data. So, when choosing this technique, think of the impact the study will have on the decision makers. Will they give credence to what they read?

Often, it is best to use the depth interview as either exploratory, to get a grassroots feel of the general sentiment, or confirmatory, to follow up on another study, such as a survey. In general, I would not rely on the depth interview alone for strategy purposes. Instead, corroborate it with more quantitative studies. Let me illustrate this point.

When my company, Tsunami Products, was forming, we conducted nondirective interviews with expert sea kayakers to ascertain what they envisioned as the ultimate sea kayak. From the information we obtained, we conducted structured depth interviews with retailers to determine if our "ultimate" sea kayak was salable, from their point of view. Later, we conducted a mail survey of kayak owners to find out what features they still wanted in a sea kayak. With the information gleaned from these studies, we obtained a composite picture of the ultimate sea kayak. We then designed, built, tested, and manufactured the ultimate sea kayak—the Tsunami X-1 Rocket.

Another pitfall of depth interviewing involves sampling—both procedure and size. Recall in the preceding chapter that the goal of sampling was representativeness. The sample must adequately represent its population or results cannot be projected beyond the few individuals interviewed. Since key individuals may be difficult to reach, researchers often rely on the snowball or judgment method of selecting samples. These are inadequate except in a pilot or exploratory study. It is best, if possible, to obtain a list of people that comprise the relevant population, and use a probability sampling method such as SRS to select interviewees. Regarding sample size, a rule of thumb you should adhere to is: use at least 30 people. Act as if you planned to use inferential statistics on the data. With 30 people, you are much more likely to at least minimally represent a homogeneous population.

Another problem lies in open-end questions, which I argued against in the previous chapter. The reasons were this: the open-end question often produces answers that are difficult to categorize or quantify (and thus are not comparable), or even to interpret with any certainty. However, the open-end question is the crux of the journalistic method. I recommend that interviewers be provided a semistructured question sequence so you, the researchers, and interviewers agree on primary and secondary questions and their sequence. Probing should be left to the discretion of the interviewer. If you opt for the nonstructured approach, you court disaster, waste time, and throw away money. Nonstructured interviewing can be equated with anarchy—it is no way to run a study or a country.

The next major problem area lies within the interviewer. In depth interviewing, the interviewer is no automaton. The interviewer possesses a great deal of power. If the interviewer is good, the results are likely to be good. If the interviewer is bad. . . Here are some interviewer problems to be aware of. First, the interviewer's personality and capabilities may not meet your needs. Make sure that interviewers are pleasant, articulate, reliable, resourceful, able to follow directions, persuasive, honest, and observant. Interview prospective interviewers to ascertain if they possess these characteristics.

Gordon (1987: 22) recommends using professional journalists to fill this role. Roller (1987: 14) recommends using professional psychologists. Journalists and psychologists function well as depth interviewers, but they cost too much. Instead, hire bright college students to do the work part-time, for a reasonable rate of pay (about one-sixth the amount a journalist or psychologist would demand). Journalism, psychology, human development, communication, and marketing majors are good candidates. Also, homemakers have been used for many years with good results in mall intercepts and house-to-house surveys. Many could be trained to conduct depth interviews.

Another problem associated with interviewers is their lack of knowledge regarding the nature of the study and what to do if problems arise. Good training and pilot testing should solve both of these problems. Even magazine feature writers must immerse themselves in a subject before they can write about it with accuracy. Training should also minimize misrecording, fudging, cheating, failing to follow directions, interactive bias, and other interviewer-based errors.

Sometimes the interview environment will wreak havoc on the interview process. The room may be too hot, the respondent is hungry or tired, or something external impedes the interview. All you can reasonably do is be aware that these things happen and try to arrange an atmosphere that is conducive to candor.

Analysis and interpretation of the results create another problem with the depth interview. Who is the appropriate person to write up the results? The interviewer? The head researcher? An independent judge? The interviewer is responsible for taking good notes or ensuring proper taping (audio or video) of the interview, and that is it. The head researcher could do the job; however, the best method (most valid and reliable) is to employ at least two independent observers to review the data separately but concurrently. They write up their own assessments, and the head researcher (or another judge) compares the two reports and prepares a composite report based on interjudge agreement. If the judges differ on key areas, they are shown the other judge's opinion, and asked to reconsider. If necessary, the judges would argue it out. Hopefully, they will reach consensus. If not, you may wish to report both opinions. Using independent judges to view the interviewer's work is like having a team of news editors reviewing a reporter's work or a group of psychiatrists discussing a clinician's diagnosis.

While we are discussing reporting, let's address the problem of sloppy reporting. For some reason, many qualitative studies suffer not only from ambiguous results, but from incomplete reporting of all procedures. Not long ago I critiqued a depth interview study for a major industrial manufacturer. The report stated that 35 qualified people were interviewed; many strong recommendations were made regarding perception of product and service. Unfortunately, many important details were omitted, such as what questions were asked, how people were selected, how the interviewer was selected and trained, what procedures were followed, and how the data were analyzed. In short, the report was inadequate and unusable except as a pilot test for a real study. My recommendation: Report all pertinent details. As noted in the last chapter, a study must be replicable. That is, another researcher following the same procedure with a similar sample should obtain equivalent results. Ensure that the study reports enough detail (including limitations) that it could be repeated. Even qualitative, subjective work should be repeatable.

Steps in Conducting Depth Interviews

Here are the steps to follow to produce a quality depth interview study. Determine if the depth interview is the best, most cost-effective way to get information you desire. Decide who will administer the study—you or an outside agency. Prepare your information needs, then develop a semistructured list of questions. Train interviewers. Pilot test procedures and the question list. Continue to refine and pilot test until error is sufficiently reduced and the study seems executable and replicable. Develop a sample frame and select respondents. Make sure these people adequately represent the population of interest.

Your next step is to follow the tested procedure and conduct the interviews. Have interviewers accurately record all information. If standardized information is needed, instruct the interviewee to complete a self-report questionnaire. This will save time and money. Develop a way to monitor interviewer performance. If personal interview is the preferred method but respondents are busy and reside across the country and time is important, consider using a telephone interview. Or, try to interview respondents in one location, such as at a convention site. These two alternatives will save money and still achieve objectives. The important thing to remember is that the data collection method must be thoroughly justified and described in the report.

Obtain independent judges to analyze and evaluate findings. Write up results; make recommendations. When writing up results, look for a pattern. Form categories whenever possible. Temper recommendations with limitations of the study. The bottom line: Ensure that your depth interviews are as scientific as possible. Retain objectivity. Do not let your study slip down into phenomenological ambiguity, else the technique loses its value.

FOCUS GROUPS

Even more than the depth interview, the focus group has emerged as the market research star during the past decade. Undoubtedly, it will enjoy prominence for another decade. However, the focus group is rampant with error. For it to continue its dominance, users of the technique need to adhere to scientific principles. These principles are discussed later, but first let's examine why the focus group is so popular today.

From a methodological standpoint, the focus group is good because it provides a central location. This allows monitoring and reduces a lot of field error. It is also relatively inexpensive on the whole. Per interview, it is more expensive than surveying, but less expensive than depth interviewing. The group setting provides more stimuli than a one-on-one setting. Participants are exposed to others' ideas and synergy can occur. Some people may feel protected in the group environment and will offer opinions more candidly than in the intense depth interview where they are always on the spot. Hy Mariampolski (1984: 21) claims that focus groups are effective because moderators can probe and challenge participants to give the "most truthful" responses. Other methodological reasons for using focus groups are presented by Hess (1968: 194) He writes that the focus group is fast, since participants are interviewed simultaneously. He adds that the focus group allows for scientific scrutiny, since several judges can observe the group.

Focus groups have many uses. Pope (1981: 187) lists categories of focus group uses. These include: suggesting hypotheses for further testing, helping structure questionnaires, looking at categories, evaluating new product concepts, generating new ideas about older products, suggesting new creative approaches, interpreting quantitative research results, and as a quick "disaster check" for promotions and other marketing mix strategies.

The primary reason the focus group is king lies in the minds of its users. Decision makers know that research is needed, yet many shy away from complex, statistics-based research in favor of the easily comprehensible focus group. Decision makers who lean on the focus group may fear number crunching, or at least are not knowledgeable of the uses of experimental designs and statistics. Sometimes these people fall prey to bad research because they do not know what is good focus group research and what is bad. Focus groups have many pitfalls; let's examine them.

Focus Group Pitfalls

Focus groups suffer all the problems of the depth interview—and more! One important difference lies in moderator versus interviewer. The moderator in a focus group needs to have all the qualities of a depth interviewer plus be able to facilitate group interaction. Hence, a good deal of the success of a focus session falls on the shoulders of the moderator. If the moderator fails, the focus group fails. If you are unsure about the qualifications needed for your focus group project, employ professional moderators with established track records.

However, it is possible to recruit exceptional students to fulfill the role of moderator. I have used bright university students as moderators with great success. The major benefits to using students are saving money and providing a nonthreatening atmosphere. Students, because they are usually youngish, do not threaten most people. Hopefully, people will open up more with a person who does not make them feel defensive. Students may not be best in all focus group situations, however, so use your best judgment.

Regardless of whom you use as moderators, they must possess excellent group facilitation skills. These skills must be tested before you put them into a real focus group. So, train your moderators in group dynamics. They should know about nonverbal behavior, groupthink (over cohesiveness), power moves, and other aspects of group communication that may surface during the session. Also, prepare them with all the details about the product being tested or the focus of the sessions. They must know as much about the concept or product as one of your sales agents would. Conduct pilot tests with the moderator, equipment, and a practice group. If you plan to conduct several groups, you may need to train two or more moderators to avoid burnout.

A big problem with focus groups centers on reluctance of participants to be candid, or even contribute. An artful and resourceful moderator can compensate for this. One thing to do is ask participants to write down their responses to each query, then instruct the moderator or participants to read the responses aloud. This encourages involvement from everyone. Another idea is to use standardized rating scales whenever possible, so everyone contributes. Finally, at the beginning of the session, the moderator can structure the process so each person contributes orally in turn.

The opposite of reluctance is dominance. Sometimes a group member or a coalition will dominate discussion. A moderator must deal with this problem early in the session or it will be doomed. Bean (1988: 6) suggests that the moderator place name cards around the table in a random manner—to discourage dominators from assuming power seats. She also suggests using subtle nonverbal cues or direct confrontation to stop the conversation hog. Another technique Bean favors is structuring the group to call on individuals so the dominator must wait his or her turn. She recommends evicting the dominator if that person is not controllable by other means.

Other problem areas revolve around recruitment and sample size. Generally, choose participants who are similar on key demographic or psychographic characteristics. This will reduce dissonance in the group and help members focus on the topic. Each focus group should have between five and nine participants. Any number lower than five is not cost-effective. Any number over nine creates control problems for the moderator. Seven is about the right number of people to form a focus group. In the research industry the number of focus groups per study averages around three or four. I recommend five groups. This will give you a sample size of about 35 people (seven persons per group). If you must divide people into subgroups (by region, usage, gender, age, or anything else important), you will need five focus groups per subgroup. Otherwise, you will not be able to extrapolate any findings to any population. As usual, I recommend that people participating in focus groups be randomly selected and randomly assigned to their group.

The agenda, or discussion guide, is yet another potential problem area. To prepare no agenda is to court disaster. To rigidly follow an agenda, no matter the mitigating circumstances, is to stifle the creative atmosphere. Solution: Carefully prepare an agenda, a guide, pilot test it, refine it, then use it—as a guide only.

Recording is another area that poses problems for focus group practitioners. Some focus sessions use two-way mirrors so the client can observe a group without contaminating the process. The problem here is that clients often seize a single statement (usually positive) and miss the whole picture. Watching a focus group unfold equates with watching a complex movie. You may not get everything the first time through. So, train clients how to view focus sessions and use recording devices. The best device to use is the television camera.

Use two cameras from differing angles. Make sure that everyone is in the picture at all times. Footage can be viewed later by the client and trained observers. Participants should be given time to acclimate to the cameras. A fixed camera operated from outside the room works best as participants tend to notice it less. Visible camera operators impose upon the session. This could cause people to ham it up or clam up.

Analysis and interpretation of focus group sessions are potentially the biggest pitfalls. Many experts recommend that the moderator and/or client analyze what occurred during the sessions. There is nothing wrong with this, but the moderator and client are not the best people to analyze results. The moderator was involved in the process and so cannot watch everyone all the time and facilitate the group effectively. The client is likely to be biased and inexperienced in evaluating focus group interaction.

Here is where videotaping sessions pays off. First, you possess a permanent record of the verbal and nonverbal interaction. From the videotape, it is easy for viewers to transcribe verbal comments from each participant for subsequent content analysis. Second, the visual aspect of the videotape allows trained observers to note nonverbal behaviors that may stand alone as communication, or complement or refute verbal interaction. Also, nonverbal communication occurs all the time as participants react to others' verbal and nonverbal interaction.

The formal analysis and interpretation of focus group data should be conducted by at least two trained observers. These observers should be competent in analyzing nonverbal behavior as well as verbal responses. The observers view copies of the videotape concurrently but separately. Their analyses are then reviewed by another researcher, who looks for interobserver agreement. This procedure will reduce subjective observer error. It is more expensive than letting the moderator write up a quick summary, but the results will be usable. Observer cost can be lowered by using college students. Focus group results that are biased and skimpy mislead decision makers. This can be quite expensive.

It is important to analyze the nonverbal component of

the interaction because one person may say "I think the product is great." Meanwhile, other participants may be turning up their noses, yawning, sticking out their tongues, snickering, raising an eyebrow, narrowing their eyes, crossing their arms and turning away, or engaging in other nonverbal behaviors that indicate that they disagree with the verbal message. Or, the person saying the product is great may do so mockingly. A mere transcript would miss this important nonverbal encoding. A client who views interaction fleetingly through a two-way mirror may also miss the complete picture.

When analyzing and interpreting focus group data, concentrate primarily on patterns of responses. That is, look at repeated comments or general agreement among participants, especially if they seem vehement about some aspect. Of course, do not overlook serendipitous comments that may be quietly uttered.

To complement videotaped verbal and nonverbal response, you may wish to use standardized rating scales before, during, or after the focus group (see Weiss 1987: 33). Or, have respondents write down their opinions and defend them in writing. Recently, electronic devices have been developed that help respondents and analysts (see Malone 1987: 38; Wheatley & Flexner 1987: 23–24). Silverstein (1988: 31) recommends using two-way focus groups when conflicting parties (e.g., doctors and patients) view the other's focus session and reach a greater understanding. Lederhaus and Decker (1987) suggest that focus group researchers use nominal group technique (NGT) to secure equal input from all participants. In NGT, ideas are generated through brainstorming, discussed, and ranked independently. Solutions are put in writing. The aformentioned techniques serve as useful variations to the focus group to help researchers obtain information that can be easily or meaningfully interpreted.

When writing up focus group results, be cautious in

making recommendations. Remember, as Karger (1987: 52) says, focus groups are for focusing, and little else. Generally, strong recommendations are not justified in focus group research. Do not be seduced.

Steps in Conducting Focus Groups

Most of the major issues regarding focus groups have been covered in this discussion, so let's briefly deal with the focus group process. First, ensure that your information needs require the focus group as a research method. Do a cost/benefit analysis and decide whether you will do the sessions in-house or through another agency. If an outside firm provides the facilities and conducts the study, ensure that you and your researchers are involved with the project. After the preliminaries are completed, develop an agenda. This is a creative endeavor involving decision makers and researchers. Then choose the moderator(s). Train moderators with the discussion guide and typical respondents. Pilot test the discussion guide, equipment, and procedures. Refine and fix elements of the focus group. Select and assign participants to the groups.

The next stage involves conducting the study. Ensure that all people, equipment, and materials are ready and that backups are available. Imagine how costly and embarrassing it would be for the participants, judges, and decision makers to show up and learn that the videographer switched on the camera and found it inoperable.

Conduct sessions the way you planned. Follow the analysis and interpretation suggestions I gave. If you diligently eliminate or reduce error, you will obtain good results from your focus group for a reasonable price. For further information on focus groups, consult the references from this chapter. You may wish to read Goldman's (1962) classic article on group depth interviews and check out Templeton's (1987) book aptly entitled, *Focus Groups.*

COMBINING DEPTH INTERVIEWS AND FOCUS GROUPS

Depth interviews and focus sessions combine artistic and scientific enterprises. There is no reason that the two methods cannot be wedded in one study. My company, Tsunami Products, did just that.

Tsunami developed an ocean kayak (the X-1) made for the rigors of the marine environment. We believed it was superior to all other kayaks in durability and performance in surf zone conditions. We decided to test the X-1 against five of the best-sellers in the industry. We planned to use the test data (if the X-1 came out on top) in our promotion program. We developed a method and instrument to compare boat performance and pilot-tested them. After refinement, we were ready to run the comparison test.

We combined the depth interview and focus group procedures and produced a hybrid method. Using judgment sampling, we recruited six advanced paddlers to test the boats and paired each with a trained proctor (students from my marketing research course). A moderator gathered testers and proctors together on a beach in San Francisco Bay and explained the testing procedures.

Each paddler rated each boat on several features, then paddled the boat in calm water and rated its performance. We then took the participants to a surfing beach and had participants test each boat in the surf and rate it. Proctors followed each boater around and recorded responses to each category. Boaters did not interact with each other during this phase of the comparison study.

Each proctor carried an observation form, which included categories of study, an importance rating scale from 1 to 5 and a rating from 1 to 5 for each category. So a boater rated the importance of each category and then rated the boat's performance in that category. Scores were obtained for each boat in each category by multiplying the category's importance rating by the boat's performance rating. Also, overall scores were obtained for each boat by summing all the judges' scores.

Additionally, each boater commented on each category and each boat's performance in that category. Qualitative comments were written down verbatim by proctors. Later, two independent judges read comments and prepared summaries of patterns from the comments. Unique comments (stated only once) were included in an appendix.

After all boats were tested, the moderator led a focus group with the six boaters. This was tape recorded and analyzed by two independent judges looking for patterns in the responses. Responses were summarized in the report and the transcript was placed in an appendix.

Our boat came out as number one overall from the quantitative part of the study and the qualitative results backed up these findings. By combining rating scales and qualitative responses one-on-one and in a focus group, we ended up with a useful study.

Naturally, the study was not perfect. Six kayakers do not represent the universe of kayakers. We should have conducted five more focus group studies and compared findings, both qualitative and quantitative, across groups. We did not have enough money to do that. Still, our findings gave us a good indication of where our boat stood compared to our competitors' boats.

Also, we should have videotaped each kayaker's structured depth interview and the focus session. Undoubtedly, this would have provided us with more useful information. We could have videotaped each boat's performance in the surf and observed it later. Again, our limited financial resources precluded this. We had to settle for what we could do. We were satisfied with the results. The study, though imperfect, was well executed and documented— and cost-effective. Moreover, the study is replicable.

The value of describing this study lies in combining methods to optimize a study. We used the depth interview and focus group. We also included a questionnaire (the observation form), which was derived from survey methodology. Finally, structured observation was used. Structured observation is described in the next chapter followed by experimentation, the most scientific method of observation.

5

Observation

If you want to know what people *do,* the best way to find out is to observe them. Using two-way mirrors, observers, and video cameras, we can observe a focus group. If we want to know how much of our premium beer consumers buy, we can employ mystery shoppers to observe purchases, or find out how many cases of our beer had been shelved, or review UPC scanner data on our beer sales, or sift through household garbage in trash dumpsters to find empty bottles. We are not forced to rely on what people say they do. These ways of knowing fall under the general rubric called observation. Some observation techniques are qualitative ethnographic studies; other are more structured and quantitative.

In this chapter, we focus on qualitative and structured observation methods. We describe each technique, discuss pitfalls, and provide guidelines for conducting studies that use observation. Let's begin with ethnographic research.

ETHNOGRAPHY

Hy Mariampolski (1988: 33) claims that ethnography is making a comeback as a marketing research tool. Ethnography is defined by Mariampolski as "the study of human behavior in its natural context." This type of research has been conducted for many years in supermarkets but has not been used much in other marketing contexts. I reviewed ten current market research texts, and ethnography was not mentioned once in any book. Across the ten texts studied, the average number of pages devoted to the entire field of observation research is four. Discussion of qualitative observation in natural setings accounts for an average of less than one page per text.

This is shameful. Here's why. Marketing managers often need to know more than what people think, they need to know what they do—in context. A focus group, a fine technique, does not allow for observing consumers' behavior in their normal environment. If you want to know how people use products, don't just read about it in a magazine, don't just ask them, watch them in their natural surroundings.

Recently, my company wanted to know how long it took to assemble several brands of folding kayaks. Rather than ask people how long it took and how they did it, we watched people assemble these boats at two kayaking symposiums. We were then able to ascertain which method worked best and which boat was easiest to assemble. Our observation technique was not sophisticated or scientific, but it was quite easy and very cheap. And it was an appropriate way to obtain the information we sought.

Qualitative field observation (ethnography) is an exploratory group of techniques that features agents (researchers) in the natural setting who observe people doing normal activities. Sometimes the agent will be a participant observer, that is, join in the behavior in the natural setting to gain a deeper understanding of the phenomena under study.

Tim Cahill, a gonzo sports writer for *Outside* magazine, is famed for partaking in the oddball sports he writes about. Cahill has hunted sea snakes, explored underground caves with scuba gear, and joined us surf kayaking. These hands-on experiences give his writing a realism and immediacy that makes for compelling reading. I have heard that research for outdoor activities for the Camel Filters man was conducted by adventurers in the wild.

These examples show that there are unlimited possibilities for this type of qualitative research. Only instead of conducting ethnographic research in the wild, the marketing researcher is likely to conduct it in the mall. Studies by Gates and Solomon (1982), Gage (1983), and Bush and Hair (1985) show that mall intercept survey research is quite popular. Malls are also an ideal location to conduct ethnographic studies. However, as you might imagine, there are problems associated with ethnographic methods. Let's examine qualitative observation weaknesses.

Ethnographic Pitfalls

One of the biggest potential problems of ethnography is that it takes too long. It often takes weeks, months, even years to fully appreciate an intact group of human beings. Jane Goodall spent years observing chimpanzee behavior in the wild. Over the years, she discovered that some of her original conclusions regarding chimpanzee behavior were premature. At first, she noted that they were peaceful vegetarians. Later, she found that chimps ate meat and were warlike. Only by observing the chimpanzees over time was she able to record cycles of behavior that the chimpanzee society went through.

If an ethnographic marketing study took as long as

Goodall's research, the cost would be enormous and the timeliness of the data would be lost. So marketing researchers must confine ethnographic studies to realistic, finite time schedules. Employing numerous observers to crash the time schedule may be a good option. Combining ethnographic data with information from other methods is another way to address the time issue. At the onset of the study, researchers must ensure that recurring, frequent behavior can be adequately observed over a reasonable time-span.

Observer bias is perhaps the major pitfall of ethnographic studies. I read three newspaper reporters' accounts of attendance figures at a free rock concert in Golden Gate Park in 1967. One reporter looked around and guessed there were at least 5,000 people at the concert. Another reporter interviewed the promoter; the promoter thought there were 15,000 people present. The third reporter asked the police officer in charge; 10,000 was the officer's estimate. Who's correct? Casual observation suffers from bias within the reporter. The reporter/researcher cannot observe everything. Selective perception means that some events that have been observed will be forgotten or distorted. A researcher in the field is inhibited by subjectivity related to prior learning. In other words, a major problem of ethnography is that other researchers may not be able to replicate previous findings with much fidelity.

There are many suitable remedies for the bias problem. First, use objective observation devices. In the free concert situation, attendance could have been monitored by a helicopter flying above. A detailed photograph could have been taken and the people could have been counted by counting a quadrant of the photo and extrapolating. Or, had tickets been collected, they could have simply been counted. If concert goers had been herded through a turnstile, they could have been counted then. Or an electronic eye could count people as they were funneled through a narrow corridor.

Another way to remedy the bias problem would be to use two or more trained observers and then compare their findings. In ethnographic research, this is the preferred solution. It is also possible to combine ethnography with surveys, depth interviews, and more structured forms of observation.

Steps in Conducting Ethnographic Marketing Research

Make sure your research questions warrant this technique. Ethnography works best in exploratory situations, or to confirm other research findings. Determine if the ethnographic approach is cost-effective. Obtain trained ethnographers to conduct the research. If possible, integrate other methods (such as depth interviews) to triangulate findings.

Set time limits and try to avoid pitfalls. Conduct research in an orderly a manner as possible. Have a trained ethnographic analyst debrief observers. When analyzing and interpreting, look for recurring patterns and search for serendipitous findings that may provide useful market information. Use caution when extrapolating. Instead of using ethnography and its incumbent vagaries, you may wish to structure observations to increase accuracy. Let's discuss structured observation.

STRUCTURED OBSERVATION

Instead of just watching and/or participating, as a reporter, spy, or ethnologist might, you might obtain more replicable observations if you overlay structure on the observation process. In structured observation, you do more than send an agent into the field to observe. Whereas ethnographic observation is exploratory in nature, structured observation is confirmatory. Structured observation may be used to test hypotheses. Kinnear and Taylor (1983: 392) opt for structured observation ". . . when the decision problem has been clearly defined and the specification of information needs permits a clear identification of the behavior patterns to be observed and measured."

To structure observation, you must develop systematic, replicable, measurable ways of observing behavior in an objective fashion. Just as in questionnaire development, specific behaviors to be observed will have to be identified beforehand, tested, and written down so trained observers can reliably obtain valid observations. The head researcher will determine whether molar (general, serial) or molecular (small, specific) behaviors will be studied. For example, in a shopping aisle, an observer might look for molar behaviors such as how many people placed a certain brand or product in their shopping carts. Or the observer may look for molecular behaviors such as how many seconds a shopper pondered brands before selecting a brand.

Other structured observation decisions must be made. Researchers will have to determine whether direct or indirect observation, or a combination is most desirable. Direct observation refers to viewing behavior as it occurs, whereas indirect observation refers to viewing behavior after it has occurred. This involves observing artifacts or physical traces. Here is an example. Suppose Jane Goodall wanted to know what chimpanzees ate. If she were to take a direct approach, she could systematically observe what they were eating through a telescope and record the foods in a journal. If Goodall were to take an indirect approach, she could collect samples of chimpanzee excrement and have them analyzed by a scatologist, who would complete a posthoc evaluation of exactly what the chimpanzees ate. A marketing example of direct observation was given when I described molar versus molecular behaviors: an observer watches shoppers place items in their carts. An indirect observation would be obtained by counting how many brand items were shelved and then counting them again after a specified time period. Both direct and indirect observation have their place. The difficult part is deciding which to use. Direct observation is better because it is direct, and seeing is believing, but often indirect observation is the easiest and cheapest way to record behavior. For example, it is easier and cheaper to follow a nuclear submarine's radiation trail by satellite than it is to tail it with another submarine.

Disguised versus undisguised observation is yet another decision area. It is better to use disguised observation in most cases, so people will not alter their behavior. Common sense dictates that people will react abnormally when they know they are being observed. For example, most people will drive the speed limit like good citizens as the state patrol car enters the highway; as soon as the trooper exits, everyone accelerates to their normal cruising speed. Of course, deviation from normal behavior under observation may not be a problem in certain instances. Most people are used to security cameras in banks and do not change their behavior. So, again, it depends upon the situation.

In our overview of structured observation, it is necessary to discuss contrived observation. In ethnology and in some marketing research situations, such as observing shoppers, behaviors occur in their natural environment. This is ideal, because we want to see true behaviors in their actual context. Sometimes this is not feasible or cost-effective. It may take a long time for an observable behavior to occur, and this may waste time and cost too much. So, it may be feasible to contrive a setting, such as a zoo or simulated store, which faithfully recreates the natural context enough to observe true behavior. For example, if we wished to observe sea life, the Monterey Bay Aquarium provides an excellent contrived environment that adequately simulates the marine environment. The trick is to cost-effectively create a simulated setting that will not adversely affect consumers' true behaviors.

Pitfalls in Structured Observation

Although structured observation alleviates some of the ambiguity and observer bias problems associated with the ethnographic approach, it also has pitfalls that must be side-stepped. Let's examine these sources of error.

One major pitfall of any observational method is that it measures the how of behavior, but not the why. Beliefs, attitudes, values, and intentions cannot be readily assessed through systematic observation alone. The solution is obvious. When why as well as how is needed, accompany observation with a survey. Surveys and observation can corroborate the findings of the other.

Structured observation opens up another area of concern—ethics. Researchers disguised as customers to test normal behaviors of clerks and sales agents may be seen as unethical, at least by those being observed. Similarly, observing unobtrusively, such as behind a two-way mirror, may be viewed as invading privacy or recording without consent. I cannot answer these questions for you, except to say that I think it is permissible ethically to observe people as long as no harm is caused. Applicable laws regarding recording should be followed.

Another problem of structured observation involves sampling. How can representativeness be assured, or even ascertained, especially in natural settings? This is difficult. In a natural setting, all that can be done is to note demographic characteristics such as age group, gender, and ethnic origin and then compare that against available statistics about the relevant population. Because of this representativeness uncertainty in natural settings, I recommend exercising caution when extrapolating beyond observations. Probably the best way to deal with the representativeness issue is to set up a simulated environment and use a probability sample of persons from your target population. If your simulation is good enough, some of the artificiality questions will be answered and you can reservedly generalize findings.

The final structured observation pitfall worth discussing, just as in ethnography, centers around observer bias. Again, I recommend employing two or more trained judges so the error is spread out, just as it is in a figure skating contest. If trained judges are given pilot-tested coding forms, observer bias will be minimized. Seymour (1987: 36) describes a "handheld, battery-powered data collector and analyzer" used by observers to record and analyze behaviors. A device such as this can aid judges in their job of observing.

Indeed, mechanical devices can augment or replace human observation. Depending upon the situation, a behavior recording device may be much more reliable and less costly than a human. The common traffic counter provides an excellent example of reliability and cost-effectiveness. Cameras, described earlier, are good recording mechanisms. Cameras (in satellites, ships, and planes) and assorted listening devices comprise the bulk of U.S. electronic defense intelligence. Our video/audio defense electronics are the best in the world.

Other recording devices are not as reliable or accurate as a camera or sound recorder. A device such as Nielsen's audimeter (and similar recorders) automatically monitors when and for how long a television is on. It even monitors which channel is on. Similar devices require viewers to punch in their code, so the measuring device can ascertain who is watching. Other television monitors sense infrared heat and guess as to how many people are in front of a television. Electronic recording devices are making rapid headway.

Unfortunately, many are expensive and flawed. In television monitoring, we still do not know if the people who are punched in and recorded as being there actually pay attention to the programs and commercials being aired. A simple ad recall telephone survey would be easier, cheaper, and provide more information about what viewers saw, what they thought of what they saw, and what they intend to do about what they saw. Do not be impressed with electronic gadgets that are not proven to be better than simpler methods.

Other electronic equipment available today includes psychogalvanometers (lie detectors), various eye movement recorders, and pupilometers. It is noteworthy that lie detector data are not admissable as evidence in a court of law. Eye movement machines record where a person looks and duration of the gaze. Pupilometers measure pupil dilation after a subject views a stimulus. The problem with all three of these electronic recording devices is that there is no valid and definitive connection with a physiological response such as sweating or pupil dilation to a mental response. For example, a subject's pupils may dilate significantly after viewing a print advertisement. The dilation by itself does not indicate anything more than "reaction" to the ad. We do not know if it was the message, the scantily clad model, or some other stimulus that caused the reaction. We also do not know why the subject reacted, or what the subject thinks about the stimulus. In the case of the eye movement recorder, just because subjects' eyes move back and forth across a page for a certain time period does not mean they comprehend what they viewed. And, with the lie detector, just because subjects sweat more when they view particular ads or are asked certain questions does not mean we can infer anything other than they "reacted physiologically" to a stimulus. We cannot and should not infer a person's mental state based upon uncontrolled physiological responses.

I have been conducting basic research on voice-pitch analysis, the measurement of pitch variation (for description and marketing research applications, see Brickman 1980; Nelson & Schwartz 1979). My colleague Jim Solomon and I (Solomon & Soares 1987) are correlating machine measurements of voice pitch variation with subjects' self-reports, trained judges' observations, and naive observers' ratings. Our preliminary research shows that there is a strong correlation among ratings of the oscilloscope, trained judges, and naive observers. However, we have found a weak correlation between machine ratings and subjects' self-reports on their vocal expressiveness. This indicates that humans differ from machine measurements in rating their own behavior. Who (or what) is correct, person or machine? AT&T, other companies, and universities are working on new ways of computer-analyzing the human voice—and its intentions. In the next ten years, marketing researchers will have access to sensitive computer analysis of many aspects of voice and speech. This will help researchers conduct more accurate studies using physiological response. Also, future physiological research will likely involve measurement of combinations of heart rate, blood pressure, hormonal levels, brain wave measurement, and other biological functions.

Meanwhile, until further validation research is completed using machines, research practitioners and users are cautioned against trusting fancy machine observations. Machine measurements should at least be correlated with other observation methods. Otherwise, you could be caught in a costly boondoggle.

Steps in Conducting Structured Observation

The steps in conducting structured observation are similar to those in ethnography. Particular emphasis should be placed on setting up a replicable, systematic, quantifiable method of collecting data. The primary advantage of structured observation is in specificity of how behavior is to be measured. Thus the measurement process must be carefully thought out, pilot-tested, and refined before observation begins. It may be necessary to conduct qualitative observation beforehand to generate structured observation criteria. Additionally, structured observations should be corroborated with other observation and/or surveys, whenever possible. Analysis should be conducted statistically and with the aid of an expert in interpretating structured observation data. By taking the time, energy, and expense to properly administer your observation study, you will save money by obtaining research information you can rely on.

Before undertaking a structured observation study or research in a natural setting, refer to these authors' works on observation: Webb et al. (1966); Wells and Lo Scuito (1966); Ray (1973); Lincoln and Guba (1985); Weller and Romney (1988). These publications will prepare you to understand and use observation techniques. With a strong understanding of observation, especially structured, systematic observation, you will be ready to undertake the most sophisticated form of marketing research—experimentation, the subject of the next chapter.

6

Experimentation

If you want to know what people *do* under specific conditions, the best way to find out is to manipulate and control the conditions and observe behavior. If you want to compare product performance or predict future consumer behavior, consider conducting an experiment. A well-executed experiment is a cost-effective way to get hard information about marketing variables you control.

Suppose we want to know which premium beer consumers *really* prefer, ours or those of our competitors. We don't just survey consumers, or put together a focus group and compare beers, or even watch them consume the stuff in a natural setting. Instead we conduct a taste test and find out, definitively. As marketing managers, we make decisions regarding the four "p's" of the marketing mix. Experimenting with various aspects of the marketing mix helps us determine product characteristics, set prices, put together the optimum media package, and commit to the best distribution channels. Consider these examples.

Regarding the product itself, we might ask ourselves, in

the beer example, what if we change the taste of our beer? Or the color? Or the shape of the bottle? Or the label? Regarding promotions, we might ask what if we use a dog as our mascot? What if we featured the dog in print ads, and/or television commercials? What if we double our advertising? Regarding pricing, we might ask what if we lower the price? Or raise it? What if we combine a change in taste with a new mascot, increased advertising, and a higher price?

These "what if?" questions reflect information needs that are foremost in the marketer's mind. As a marketer, you want to make causal statements such as "Beer sales have increased 5 percent this quarter as a direct result of ____" (insert: advertising, pricing, new packaging, drought). It is essential that you be correct or large sums of money may be lost. Experimentation, the most sophisticated of all marketing research methods, is the way to decidedly and inexpensively address cause and effect.

Many marketing researchers would disagree when I claim that experimentation is cost-effective. The consensus seems to be that experimentation is complex and therefore must be expensive. This is not the case. A carefully constructed, parsimonious experiment is more complex than survey or focus group research, but is often the most cost-effective form of research in the long run. A good experiment requires more input and skill in the planning stage, consumes about the same amount of energy in the execution stage, and often takes less effort in the data analysis phase. Twenty-five years ago, experimentation was seldom used in marketing research situations, even though it was popular among behaviorists. Now the experimental method is beginning to garner the attention it deserves in marketing research circles. More companies experiment today than ever before. Some experimentation is a capricious waste of time and money, such as extensive test marketing, but on the whole, a tight experiment serves as a powerful tool for sharp marketers with big decisions to make. I predict that experiments will become commonplace among marketing researchers in the near future.

Although I highly recommend experimental methods to answer many important research questions, they demand a lot of savvy, alertness, and attention to detail to get your money's worth. In this chapter, experimentation is explained, pitfalls are described—along with ways to overcome them—and detailed procedures are provided.

THE COMPONENTS OF AN EXPERIMENT

According to Aaker and Day (1983: 247), an experiment "involves an intervention by the observer beyond that required for measurement." Experiments also require all the careful attention to procedure discussed in aforementioned reseach methods. Experiments are used to establish causality—a causal relationship between manipulated variables and measurement variables. Experiments are used to produce data to test hypotheses—carefully worded statements about relationships among variables.

Experiments follow the scientific method. That is, they are structured, systematic, precise, and replicable. The aim of science is to understand, predict, and control. Naturally, experiments dealing with humans are subject to more error than in the physical sciences, due to humans' high variability. Thus it is more difficult to conduct an experiment using humans than metals. All experiments dealing with human behavior share one thing in common; they examine the effect of one variable upon another. Let us now examine experimental designs.

DESIGNS

When discussing experimental design, the classic reference is Campbell and Stanley's (1963) *Experimental and*

Quasi-experimental Designs for Research. I base design description on their work. (By the way, their book is straightforward, clear, and complete. Acquire it for your company library.) Campbell and Stanley identify three basic classes of experimental designs: true experimental, quasi-experimental, and pre-experimental. Before examining each type, let's look at aspects of design that are common to all design types.

Experiments use standard notation (see Banks 1965). Some symbols often used in experimental designs include the following:

O stands for an observation, or measurement. An observation/measurement variable is called a dependent variable. The variable is "dependent" because a subject's (participant's) score is dependent upon causal influences from independent variables.

X stands for a level of an experimental treatment. A "treatment" may be a new vaccine, or in a marketing context, a type of advertisement. So, in pharmacological research we may experiment with four treatment levels of a painkilling local anesthetic: $X1$—Supercaine (our new product), $X2$—Xylocaine, $X3$—Novacaine, and $X4$—a placebo, to see which kills pain the best. A variable such as 'X' (Drug Type), is called a treatment variable. Treatment variables are independent variables. Classification variables are also independent variables but are not manipulated like a treatment variable. An example of a classification variable would be sex type, or any demographic, behavioral, or psychographic variable with arbitrary classifications or categories.

R stands for randomization, or randomized assignment of a subject to a treatment group. The *R* indicates that the design is true experimental. Individual error is spread out among treatment levels.

So, a sample design might look like this:

$$R \quad X1 \quad O1$$
$$R \quad X2 \quad O1$$
$$R \quad X3 \quad O1$$
$$R \quad X4 \quad O1$$

In the aforementioned drug-type experiment, the four levels of X would indicate the four treatment types, and the O's should represent observation or measurement. In this case, let's imagine a measurement called a painometer rating that physiologically measured sensation. Whereas the X varies, the O score is dependent on subjects' scores within each treatment condition. The *R* indicates that subjects were randomly assigned to each condition from a common pool. This design is true experimental and represents the simplest and most used true experiment. We could change Drug Type to Ad Type, or Price, or distribution channel, or any marketing mix variable. That's the beauty of this design. Let's examine more true experimental designs.

True Experiments

The above design is called an after-only with control (or posttest-only with control). It is my favorite design and the one I recommend for most experimental research contexts. It eliminates many forms of error (more on that later), it is easy to plan and execute, and it is cost-effective, compared to other true experimental designs and many quasi-experimental designs. Before discussing the other designs (they have their place), let's look into characteristics common to all true experiments.

First, *all* experiments share these traits: objectivity, measurement, precision, reliability and validity, cause and effect, hypothesis testing, quantitativeness, probability, avoiding error, systematic procedures, and comparison. Experiments are scientific, more than other marketing research methods. Additionally, true experiments evidence three more characteristics: manipulation, control groups, and randomization. Let's discuss these.

Objectivity is the hallmark of experimentation. Personal

biases are put aside to address the problem at hand scientifically, rather than critically. We can be subjective after the study is written. Measurement, precise measurement, is necessary if we plan to repeat the study. Replication, repeating experiments, establishes reliability for the procedure and validity for the results. In other words, we cannot say that our study proves anything if the results cannot be replicated. Replication is seldom done in pure behavioristic research conducted at universities. Worse, experiments are hardly ever replicated in marketing research. And this is sad. For how will we know if our results are "true" if we cannot repeat the experiment and obtain equivalent results? It is often worth the seemingly extra expense to replicate an experiment, especially if major cash outflows will be expended based upon the results. At the very least, an extensive pilot study should be conducted before the actual study, thus the actual study in effect replicates the pilot study. Then we may obtain evidence that refutes or supports our hypotheses.

Cause and effect and hypothesis testing are two other elements common to all experiments. By cause and effect, I mean we seek to predict future behavior based upon our results. This is powerful—and risky. We test hypotheses (formal statements made about the relationship between independent and dependent variables), or at least address research questions. Hypotheses are testable because we use numbers. Thus, our results must be quantifiable. We test hypotheses with statistics and then make statements concerning our results based on statistical probabilities.

Statistical algorithms make allowance for random error. However, extraneous error cannot be accounted for statistically. So, all experiments are designed and executed to avoid, reduce, measure, or account for errors, biases, contamination, environmental influences, and the like. This is why systematic procedures are designed and executed precisely. All variables, independent and dependent, are operationalized. That is, their operations are stated in clear, measurable, repeatable terms. A recipe for a lemon meringue pie serves as a good analogy. If the directions are wrong in any respect, your pie will be markedly different from the famous chef's.

Finally, experiments compare things. Usually, they compare different groups. So, in our drug type example, Xylocaine and Novacaine serve as valid comparisons with Supercaine, the drug under study. All true experiments compare effects. This is done scientifically through manipulation of treatment variables such as Drug Type. A classification variable such as Sex Type is not manipulated; people are either male or female. Thus Sex Type may compare the two sexes, but nothing is manipulated.

Although comparison with other drugs is good, it may not be good enough. Perhaps other factors are working that may confound or cancel the effects of comparison groups, or even be the primary effect on the dependent variable. Thus in true experiments the control group is used to check to see if outside influences are effecting measurement.

There are two types of control groups: do something and do nothing. A placebo, as used in the Drug Type experiment, is a do something control group. Here, control group participants "do" all that those in the experimental conditions (e.g., Xylocaine, Supercaine), do, except those in the placebo condition receive no stimulus (drug), and instead are given sugar water, or the like. The purpose is to ascertain if effects on the dependent variable (painometer rating) are due to comparison groups or something else. If we suspected that the mere presence of researchers (or doctors) causes pain to go away, we would add in X5, a do nothing control group. This group would be measured with the painometer at the same time as the other four groups, but would not go through the procedure of receiving treatment. Thus if bedside manner were an outside cause, the do nothing control group would differ significantly from the other groups on the painometer rating.

True experiments are also characterized by random assignment (R). Subjects are randomly assigned to each condition, thereby spreading out random variation common in people and eliminating researcher assignment bias. If any of these three characteristics are missing (manipulation, control groups, or random assignment), then you do not have a true experimental design.

In addition to the after-only with control group, there are two other principal true experimental designs: the before/after with control, and the Solomon four-group. The before/after with control (also called the pretest/posttest with control) looks like this in its simplest form:

$$R \; O1 \; X1 \; O2$$
$$R \; O1 \; X2 \; O2$$
$$R \; O1 \; X3 \; O2$$
$$R \; O1 \; X4 \; O2$$

The notation symbols are the same as in the after-only design, except there are two measurements, a pretest and a posttest (O1, O2). The pretest (O1) offers a score on the dependent variable that can be compared with the posttest score. The pretest feature is useful if prior data on each subject is necessary. In the Drug Type study, we may wish to obtain pretest measurement using the painometer and compare these data with posttest results. In fact, we could extend the design to several observations:

$$R \; O1 \; X1 \; O2 \; O3 \; O4$$
$$R \; O1 \; X2 \; O2 \; O3 \; O4$$

This is called a time-series with control group. Time is measured from left to right. The problem with the pretest/posttest type of designs is pretest learning. The testing effect occurs when subjects "learn" from the pretest and thus experience a differential score on the posttest than they would have had they not taken the pretest. One way to solve this is to select subjects who come from populations with baseline data already accrued for that population. Thus in our Drug Type study, typical painometer scores are known, and these data are used as a general base to test the effects of the sensation-deadening drugs. So, the pretest/posttest design is rejected in favor of the more parsimonious and time-based-error-free posttest only with control.

Another option available, assuming that you must have the pretest data but want to avoid and measure possible learning effects, is to use the randomized Solomon Four-group design. This design combines a pretest/posttest with control and a posttest only with control. It looks like this:

$$R \; O1 \; X1 \; O2$$
$$R \; O1 \; X2 \; O2$$
$$R \; O1 \; X3 \; O2$$
$$R \; O1 \; X4 \; O2$$

$$R \quad X1 \; O2$$
$$R \quad X2 \; O2$$
$$R \quad X3 \; O2$$
$$R \quad X4 \; O2$$

As you can imagine, there are variations on this theme, all expensive. The Solomon design, although the most thorough, is also the costliest and should be avoided. It should be avoided for another reason, and that is error. Although time-based errors are measured and controlled in the Solomon design, the experiment risks more contamination due to experimental setting and general environment errors. This is due to the Solomon design's complexity. As I advised earlier, the posttest only with control is the most used true experimental design in the world—and is the one I recommend for simplicity, reduction of error, and cost efficiency. Of course, you may opt for a design that differs from a true experiment, according to your specific research needs.

Quasi-experimental Designs

To obtain a true experiment, the researcher must manipulate treatment variables, use control groups, and randomly assign subjects to treatment conditions. Often, this can be done only in a controlled environment, a laboratory. Some causal relationships are best tested in a laboratory setting. Other marketing research questions can best be addressed in the field, where the artificiality associated with laboratories is lessened. But if you conduct an experiment in stores, it will be difficult to account for extraneous variation. It may be impossible to randomly assign people to control groups, or even to use control groups. A causal study that lacks control groups or randomization is quasi-experimental.

The quasi-experiment is a reasonable alternative to the true experiment when generalizability of findings to target populations is the goal and the artificiality of the lab would markedly detract from that goal. It is important that the decision maker and researcher carefully determine if the quasi-experiment is substantially better, because quasi-experiments are often more expensive than true experiments, more difficult to administer, and subject to much more error. It may be more cost-effective to simulate the real environment in the laboratory. For example, if you are interested in testing various shelving schemes, you could create simulated store aisles easier than you could rearrange real store aisles. Here is a more dramatic example. It is easier, cheaper, and safer to simulate space flight when training astronauts than it is to send them into space. The space shuttle simulator provides sufficient realism.

If you decide the quasi-experiment is the only way to go, here is a suitable design, called a multiple time series design (see Banks 1965: 44):

$$O1 \ O2 \ O3 \ X1 \ O4 \ O5 \ O6$$
$$O1 \ O2 \ O3 \ X2 \ O4 \ O5 \ O6$$
$$O1 \ O2 \ O3 \ X3 \ O4 \ O5 \ O6$$

Here we have three levels of X, two comparison groups, and one do-nothing control group. We have three pretests and three posttests. Subjects in the three sets of observations are not randomly assigned; hopefully, subjects match on key characteristics. Otherwise, this and other time series designs are practically worthless.

Pre-experimental Designs

Assuming you can match subjects, it may not suit your research needs to conduct a quasi-experiment. You may wish to study causal relationships that do not require a set of expensive pretests and posttests to give you needed results. In this case, consider the pre-experiment, which is similar to the quasi-experiment in that conditions for true experimentation are not met, but the pre-experiment is easier to do—and often much cheaper.

Pre-experiment examples include the one-shot case study (X1 O1), in which one treatment (such as Supercaine) is administered to a group of people. Hopefully, these people will have been randomly selected from the target population. If premeasurement is needed, consider the one-group pretest/posttest (O1 X1 O2). Notice that these two designs omit a control group. The status quo can count as a pseudo-control group if you are testing a new format (e.g., a new sales program) with an old format still in existence. This design is symbolized as

$$X1 \quad O1$$
$$X2 \quad O1$$

where X1 is the new sales program and X2 is the current program. This design is called a static-group comparison. A time series without any control group (even a status quo group) is often considered quasi-experimental, although it is unclear why. It is just a glorified and extended one-group pretest/posttest. More pretests and posttests do not automatically improve a design. More tests and observations mean more error and cost. Plus, an experiment drawn out over time is more complex and requires more administrative effort. This militates against a key principle of science—parsimony. Research questions should be phrased, studied, and interpreted in as simple a manner as possible, without demeaning the validity of the study. In the short and long run, function is more important than form.

Complex Designs

Although I argue for simplicity in design, sometimes complex designs are actually more parsimonious. Consider the factorial design, where more than one independent variable is of interest to marketing management. Would it not be easier and more cost-effective to combine two or more experiments and optimize personnel, resources, and subjects gathered? In many cases, the answer is yes. Use the factorial design for two purposes. The first purpose centers on examining the "interaction" of two or more independent variables on a common dependent variable. This is considered the ideal purpose for using factorial experiments. We would look for meaningful relationships on dependent variable scores where levels of independent variables interact together. For instance, in the Drug Type experiment, we might also believe that males and females differ significantly on painometer readings. So, we might construct a 4 × 2 matrix, a two-way factorial, of Drug Type by Sex Type, and see how each sex experiences sensation in each of the four drug conditions. We might hypothesize that females in the Supercaine condition would feel the least sensation.

We could also treat each independent variable as a separate experiment and not look at interaction. So, we would make hypotheses about drug effects and sex differences, but not about their interaction. We would focus only on main effects of each independent variable on the dependent variable. On the surface this makes sense, especially when you have no reason to believe that independent variables would interact with each other. But what if they do? What would you do? Most experts agree that in the presence of significant interaction, ignore main effects. Usually, I would agree. But what if you cannot explain the reason for the interaction and you have significant main effects? Then you are in a quandary. If there is no reasonable explanation you can give for the significant interaction, and would not predict one, then perhaps you do not have a complete understanding of your independent variables. Worse, error could be the cause of the interaction. If this happens, examine everything closely and view results with suspicion.

You can design factorial experiments to include more than two independent variables. Suppose your previous research showed that music had no effect on painometer readings. You may wish to include that variable also. You might have two levels: 1 = rock and roll, 2 = no music.

Here we would have three independent variables, Sex Type, Drug Type, and Music. So you would experiment with sex, drugs, and rock and roll.

This factorial experiment would be a three-way design, represented like this: $4 \times 2 \times 2$ (rows, columns, layers), four levels of Drug Type, two levels of Sex Type, and two levels of Music. These levels together form cells. If we multiply $4 \times 2 \times 2$, we get 16 cells. This is a manageable design. We need a minimum of 30 people per cell to obtain adequate power to detect significant differences; 16 cells times 30 subjects equals 480. We need a minimum of 480 people (divided equally between male and female) for this study. Actually, we need more people than 480, because some will drop out. The point is, 480 subjects is parsimonious. But what if we decided to try two more types of music, such as classical and jazz; then how many people would we need? In a $4 \times 2 \times 4$ design, we would obtain 32 cells and would need a minimum of 960 people, thereby doubling expense, complexity, and chances of error.

What if we wanted to add another independent variable to the design? Then we would have an ungainly experiment. Therefore, I advise the following regarding design complexity. Use a factorial design only if the situation truly warrants it. Keep the number of variables and the levels of each to a minimum. Use a randomized, posttest-only with control design, if possible. In other words, keep it simple. Advise researchers conducting your experiment to heed these words. Resist the temptation to use complex, quasi-experimental field experiments.

There are other complex designs available for special purposes. These include nested designs (experiments within experiments), randomized block designs (where certain extraneous effects are blocked out), and counter-balanced treatment designs such as the Latin Square (in which no interaction is assumed and you wish to simplify higher-order factorial experiments by using a reduced number of subject groups and treatment combinations). Each special design is potentially cost-effective and has its place in marketing research contexts. A word of warning, however. Nested and Latin Square designs are difficult to interpret; there is a dearth of computer programs to assist you in statistical calculations for these designs. If you must use one of these designs, obtain an expert in design to assist. Randomized blocks save on the number of subjects needed, due to blocking. But note that blocking effects can be calculated after the study with analysis of covariance statistics. And if you are wrong on your blocking strategy, you will lack enough subjects for adequate statistical analysis. Again, plan and execute simplicity.

One other experimental design is worth noting here— the repeated measures design. It differs from time series, where several observations are made on each level of the treatment variable. With a repeated measures design, the same subjects are used across all treatment levels, rather than each subject being assigned to a separate level and then monitored. The advantage to the repeated measures design is fewer subjects. Theoretically, thirty subjects could be used across four treatment levels and this would equate with 120 subjects in a normal one independent variable design with four levels. Fewer subjects means lower cost. However, the repeated measures design can be used only when the testing effect can be effectively eliminated. Repeated measures would be appropriate for a product or taste test, but inappropriate for the Drug Type experiment. Once a subject had been in one drug condition, this would effect his or her responses in the other conditions. If you use a repeated measures design, be sure to alternate the order of treatments to reduce primacy (first treatment has greatest effect), or recency (last treatment has greatest effect) error. And record the order each subject is in to later test for an order effect.

PITFALLS OF EXPERIMENTAL RESEARCH

I have discussed several weaknesses inherent in experimental designs, but the nature of experimentation demands that you closely attend to the enemy—error. Errors that plague experiments impact all types of research. So the lengthy discussion offered here will apply to some degree to all research methods described in earlier chapters. Errors in experimentation can be divided into five major classes: design related errors, experimenter errors, environmental errors, experimental context errors, and miscellaneous errors. Let us discuss these errors and how to address them.

Design Errors

First, no matter how hard a researcher tries, it is not possible to always eliminate extraneous variability. You can recognize likely sources of error and plan a design that will avoid or control error. You can include the error into the design as an independent variable and measure it. You can monitor error; you can report it. You can maximize the potency of treatment variables to strongly effect dependent variables. You can pilot test your design and procedures to detect contamination. You can replicate your experiment directly and with modifications. Because some nonsampling error is unavoidable when studying human behavior, you should exercise caution in making causal claims based upon the results of your study. In other words, avoid advertising hype such as "A major study *proves* that our product eliminates cavities in infant rats."

Campbell and Stanley (1963: 8) identified eight major "sources of invalidity" for research designs. These are covered in almost all modern marketing research texts. I mention them now only because they are so important.

The first is history, events that occur outside the experimental setting that may effect results over time. This error is most egregious in time series designs, but can even effect one-shot designs that take a long time to administer. The second jeopardizing factor, maturation, is related to history, but refers to changes in subjects over time; they mature. The third factor is testing, the learning effect of the pretest. Instrumentation or instrument decay (or instrument enhancement), in which the measurement device, scale, or rater change over time or between subjects, is the fourth rival hypothesis. Statistical regression, or subjects' regression toward the mean or median in posttests, is the fifth source of error. Selection of static groups is the sixth jeopardizing factor. Here, subjects for various treatment levels are recruited differentially. Mortality comprises the seventh factor that threatens the internal validity (design adequacy) of an experiment. Mortality refers to subjects dropping out of the study before its completion. Interaction between jeopardizing factors is the last source of invalidity. They also list a few factors that effect generalizability of findings that relate to design choice and are represented by interactions of the other jeopardizing factors.

Campbell and Stanley and others claim that all true experiments and many quasi-experiments control these factors. I disagree. Time-based errors such as history, maturation, testing, and mortality cannot always be adequately controlled (and are certainly not automatically controlled) with randomized pretest/posttest designs or with time series designs, regardless of whether control groups are used. Here is why.

History, intervening between measurements, is not controlled just by simultaneously observing treatment and control groups. True, it is necessary to conduct all observations of treatment levels simultaneously to avoid intersubject communication. However, simultaneous execution in no way precludes history effects. Events that might affect subjects' scores could occur between measurements and affect members of control groups differently than people in treatment groups. Ordinarily, researchers rely on events to equivalently affect groups. Perhaps this is so. But unless the researcher watches subjects or maintains tight control over subjects' whereabouts, activities, and exposure to events, the researcher has really no idea how subjects may be affected. The same is true for maturation. These two jeopardizing factors are even more out of control in the field. The more observations you make and the longer you wait between observations, the more unmonitored history and maturation could occur. The bad part about these insidious errors is that the researcher would have no sure way of knowing if or how subjects were affected by time-based errors.

Here is my advice for addressing history and maturation. Don't assume that the design will automatically control the problem. Insert a question mark for these factors and don't overstate your findings. If you must use a time series design, minimize the number of observations and keep the time between observations as short as possible. Conduct a detailed manipulation check after the final posttest to ascertain if subjects were contaminated by these factors. If you follow these steps, you will also tackle the other two time-based factors, testing and mortality. Ask questions about testing during the manipulation check. Forecast the percentage of subjects that will drop out for various reasons and increase your sample size enough to account for attrition.

Experimenter Errors

Head researchers and experimenters contribute to the error equation. Researchers must exercise rigor in planning and executing all phases of an experiment. Researchers must ensure that experimenters are trained properly in conducting the experiment. Researchers must evaluate results properly and carefully phrase conclusions and recommendations. These careful phrasings protect everyone, not just researchers' flanks. For example, the head researcher in charge of the Coca-Cola taste tests, (nearly 200,000 of them, according to a 1985 *Newsweek* article), should have (and probably did) limit recommendations to the results at hand. The Coke conclusion and recommendation should (and probably did) read: "Subjects significantly prefer sweet colas over the classic Coke formula [conclusion]. These preferences should be considered in future marketing and production decisions [recommendation]." The head researcher should not have and probably did not recommend that Coca-Cola reformulate and remarket Coke based on taste test results alone. Why change a good thing (Coke—the market leader) just because number two (Pepsi) correctly claims that subjects prefer the sweeter taste of Pepsi. The decision makers at Coca-Cola did not look at the whole picture; they acted on impulse. They forgot that brand loyalty to capricious products such as soft drinks is based upon perceived image, not reality. Lesson learned: Stick to the results.

Experimenters and proctors (those who physically carry out the experiment) serve as sources of error. Experimenters may fail to follow the procedures correctly, either through ignorance, negligence, or deliberate omission or commission of acts. These errors can be reduced by carefully selecting experimenters, lecturing them on ethics, thoroughly training them (including pilot testing), monitoring their actions, and including them as part of the design. Ideally, you want experimenters to look and act in a consistent, standard way.

Some experimenter errors that are more subtle and insidious include the halo effect and the experimenter expectancy effect. The halo effect occurs when an experimenter first meets subjects. The experimenter may unconsciously act in differential ways to subjects based on first impressions. The experimenter may perceive one subject as an angel (hence, the halo), and another as a devil. By the way, all participants in an experiment are subject to the halo effect. The best way to deal with this is to train experimenters to be aware of it and to maintain objectivity.

The experimenter expectancy effect occurs when experimenters subconsciously, covertly, and subtly communicate their performance expectations to subjects. This error is most pronounced in time series achievement studies, when the experimenter and subjects interact a lot over time. Again, proper training of experimenters is the best solution. Also, you can design a "double blind" experiment, in which experimenters or proctors are unaware of the treatment condition they are administering.

Another error regarding experimenters centers on their physical characteristics. This includes age, sex, race, attire, and physical attractiveness. As a general rule, you should only include experimenters with characteristics that will minimally influence subjects' responses.

Environment Errors

The physical environment (e.g., a theater, lab rooms, stores) contributes to error. All areas in which an experiment takes place must be comparable with each other. Otherwise, environmental influences such as temperature, lighting, air quality, furniture, and size and location of the testing area may differentially affect groups. Ensure that testing areas are similar. If they are not, report it, monitor it, and possibly incorporate environment differences in the design to test for contamination. Ideally, testing areas should be more than uniform; they should also be comfortable. In other words, try to provide rooms that are just right, not too hot or cold. You don't want subjects responding to experimental stimuli in a way that differs from how the target population would. This brings us to the next general source of error—the experimental context.

Context Errors

No matter how comfortable and realistic the testing place is, subjects may still react to the testing environment itself if they are aware that they are being tested. Testing awareness problems result from subjects' reactions to being tested. Here are a few of the many potential errors resulting from testing awareness.

The first source of error is the Hawthorne effect. This occurs when subjects act differently than they normally do just because they are involved in an experiment. Thus their behavior may improve or get worse. More specific Hawthorne-type error includes social desirability, evaluation apprehension, and the boomerang effect.

Social desirability, normally associated with survey responses, also occurs in experiments. Here, subjects know they are under observation and act in the socially correct way, rather than the way they normally would. There are instruments available today that can test for social desirability. Administer these after the experiment.

Evaluation apprehension is observation nervousness, which may affect subjects' behaviors, especially autonomic physiological responses such as flushing, heart rate, blood pressure, galvanic skin response, voice steadiness, and breathing. The obvious solution to this problem is to calm subjects' apprehension. This is easier said than done. Here is what to do: Before the experiment, relax subjects by giving them time to acclimate to the surroundings, people, and tasks. Train experimenters to be low key. After the experiment, ask subjects questions pertaining to their apprehension and how it affected their behavior.

The boomerang effect occurs when subjects purposefully attempt to alter their normal behavior to foul up the experiment. This effect can be quite serious, if subjects behave wrongly yet do not let on that they have done so. There is not much that can be done about this, except to monitor subjects for disruptive behavior during the selection process and the experiment. Also, after the experiment, when administering the manipulation check, ask if subjects' altered their behavior for any reason and ask subjects what they thought the true purpose of the experiment was and how they felt about that. If you have reason to suspect a subject's behavior, dump the results later. Hopefully, the subject will not interfere with the experiment itself. If this occurs, deal with it the best you can. Unfortunately, one bad subject can ruin an entire experiment. Imagine the outcome if a subject shouted out a derogatory remark during the experiment. Again, well-planned and executed procedures with trained experimenters can reduce this possibility.

These are some of the problems that face experimenters when subjects know they are under observation. So, the researcher's choice is to administer the experiment in the field, with hidden or unobtrusive observation so subjects act normally, and face uncontrolled environmental factors, or construe an experimental setting that controls unwanted extraneous contamination but is artificial. By artificial I mean contrived, unrealistic, where subjects know they are being observed for some purpose.

Many marketers choose the realistic environment with its incumbent contamination, but there is a good cause for the simulated environment. Tucker defends the laboratory experiment (Tucker et al. 1981: 152). In responding to the "lab experiments are not relevant to the real world" argument, he writes:

In the real-life situation small but important differences are likely to go unnoticed—to be literally buried with the hundreds of ongoing events. In the laboratory the researcher can observe with greater precision. A principle discovered in an experimental situation can be injected into more natural, real-life situations to test its effect under those conditions.

Charlton and Ehrenberg (1976: 152) conducted a brand choice experiment and concluded that "The experiment also confirms earlier findings that buyer behavior under semi-artificial conditions resembles that in real life."

So, a compromise between the laboratory and the real world is possible. I advise, whenever possible, to test in the laboratory because of precision and cost efficiency, then extend the study to the real world.

Miscellaneous Experimental Errors

There are numerous other sources of error that plague experiments. One is the "law of the instrument." Sometimes researchers use a particular measurement simply because they are familiar with it. The focus should not be on the measurement instrument, but on the research problem. To avoid this, ascertain the problem first, then review the literature for valid and reliable measurement instruments. Avoid constructing your own observation/measurement procedures that may lack validity and/or reliability.

In addition to the aforementioned errors, experimentation suffers from all errors you would encounter using observation, surveys, or focus groups. So, be aware of these additional jeopardizing factors and plan and execute your experiment in a high fidelity manner. Your efforts will be rewarded with high quality results that you can predict with. Now let's go over the major stages in executing experiments.

STEPS IN EXECUTING AN EXPERIMENT

Although each experiment is unique, all go through similar procedures. Here I list ten key steps in conducting taste tests (say for cola). These steps would also be appropriate for just about any experiment.

1. State the problem. Identify colas to be tested. Decide if experimentation is the most cost-effective method to address the problem.
2. Formulate hypotheses and research questions. Make predictions about the relationships between measurement variables (taste rankings and ratings) and the independent variables (treatment variables such as cola brands or formulations and classification variables such as sex and age group). Derive hypotheses from secondary research, focus groups, company experience and opinion, and pilot studies.
3. Construct an experimental design. Construct a true experiment (at least for a taste test, where realistic settings are immaterial). Quasi-experiments may be appropriate for other types of experiments. Consider repeated measures designs to allow subjects to rate and rank all brands and to save money. Make your design minimize as much error as possible.
4. Operationalize dependent and independent variables. For the dependent variable, decide how taste preference will be measured (e.g., observation, physiological responses, rankings, rating scales, paired product comparisons, or a combination of the above). Use dependent variables that have a history of use, reliability, and validity. Cross-validate mea-

surements (such as rankings) with other dependent variables (such as ratings). For independent variables, determine how many treatment and classification variables are needed, and how many levels of each. Remember, choose as few variables and levels as possible to optimally represent factors of interest. This will make the experiment simpler and a better cost value.

5. Devise a sampling plan. This includes selection and assignment to treatments. Although most behavioral scientists are good at random assignment, they forget random selection. Concisely define the population of interest and stratify based on key segmentation variables such as cola consumption, age categories, activities. For a taste test, stratified or simple random sampling are the appropriate sampling procedures to use. Choose an optimal sample size. Coca-Cola chose nearly 200,000 people, which is at least 190,000 too many, no matter how many variables of interest they were measuring. A better way to determine sample size is to ensure that every cell contains at least thirty subjects. This will enable you to use any hypothesis test with moderate power to detect significant differences if they exist. To be safe, you should assign forty-five to sixty people per cell, to account for attrition.

6. Set up data analysis procedures. Put together a computer codebook, which lists all variables and their respective columns. Set up dummy tables and figures, and plan hypothesis tests. This will ensure that you don't conduct the experiment to find that you do not have the capacity to analyze your results.

7. Construct an experimental plan. Prepare participant and experimenter activities and instructions. Write a cover story, which is a preamble that gives subjects a plausible reason for conducting the experiment without spilling the beans as to the true nature of the study. Devise a manipulation check to be performed directly after the experiment. The manipulation check is a short questionnaire that asks participants what they knew or hypothesized about the purpose of the study, and whether they believe they responded in a normal

way for them. Plan for and secure all rooms, equipment, and materials for the experiment. Make sure you obtain backups and make contingency plans for unexpected occurrences. Pilot test and rehearse all procedures. Adjust plans as necessary, and pilot test and rehearse again.

8. Conduct the experiment. Follow the experimental plan to the letter. Monitor and record all that occurs during the experiment. After the experiment, administer the manipulation check, debrief participants and experimenters.

9. Analyze data. Review, edit, and code all observations and measurements. Discard faulty observations. Follow the data analysis plan. Evaluate and interpret results (see Chapter seven).

10. Write results. Include a detailed methods and limitations section, so others can replicate your work and assess its value. Include conclusions and recommendations, but do not extrapolate beyond the findings. Append ancillary tables and figures (see Chapter eight).

If you follow the steps outlined here, you will likely experience success when experimenting. Also, since experimentation is so rigorous, if you get it down, you will find that all your other research projects benefit with the increased attention to precision.

You probably have surmised that I am a big fan of experimentation, and why not? It is the best way (usually) to test marketing mix variables, the only tools a marketer controls. Why not determine which promotion strategy, or product feature, or price is best? Good decisions are necessary. And experimentation need not be expensive to be good. And as Cox and Enis (1969: 109) wrote: Experimentation works! Use it.

To prepare yourself to understand and use experimentation, take a course in experimental methods in psychology from a local university. I teach experimentation in my undergraduate and MBA research courses. Contact marketing professors at your university to see if they offer experimental methods in their research courses. Occasionally, the American Marketing Association or other organization or company offers seminars and workshops on experimentation. Check these out.

In addition to those already mentioned in this chapter, here are a few other classic books you should acquire for your company marketing library: *Experimental Design in Psychological Research* (1968) by Edwards; *Experimental Design: Procedures for the Behavioral Sciences* (1968) by Kirk; *Experimental Psychology* (1978) by McGuigan; and *The Logic of Scientific Discovery* (1959) by Popper. Read these books and you will obtain a detailed understanding of experimental procedures with human subjects.

7
Data Analysis

No matter which type of study you perform, you must analyze data. Your data may be qualitative (no numbers) or quantitative. In either case, several things must be done to adequately address the data. These include reviewing and editing data, entering it into a computer, and performing proper data analysis procedures, often with computer programs. Reducing error, presenting data adequately and clearly, and doing it cost-effectively are the three goals of data analysis.

In this chapter we meet these three goals. We begin with editing qualitative and quantitative data. Qualitative data analysis considerations are discussed, followed by quantitative data analysis. Quantitative analysis is further broken down into basic statistics and multivariate statistics. The chapter ends with classic, current, and future uses of computer programs to analyze data. Detailed descriptions of statistical techniques and all algorithms are omitted; these are covered in statistical texts. Here we discuss some aspects and applications of the most commonly used statistics in marketing research, along with rules of thumb for using them.

EDITING

Whether your data be qualitative or quantitative, a comprehensive and systematic process of reviewing its usefulness is needed. If you developed a data analysis plan and designed your measurement forms according to that plan, then editing will be easy. If you did not, editing is apt to cause you a major headache, because your questionnaires, observation forms, or interview notes will not be set up to facilitate review and analysis. Let's review the important and often glossed over stage of editing.

Editing Qualitative Data

Qualitative data may be photos and field notes from an ethnographic study. Or, it may be a series of open-end questions from a survey, depth interview, or focus group. Your data may be audio or videotape. If projective techniques were used, your data may even be drawings. At any rate, with qualitative data, you lack prearranged codes to make editing and analysis easy (otherwise your data would be at least nominally quantitative). Editing will take a long time. Here is yet another instance in which qualitative studies, which are seemingly straightforward and inexpensive, are in reality vague and costly—at least to edit.

When reviewing for usefulness, there are a few things you can do. Whichever medium your data are on, put aside (reject) all notes, forms, pictures, videotapes that do not address the information needs you developed at the beginning of the study. This will probably cut your remaining job in half. Second, put all remaining text and other media in your computer. Densus Corporation and other companies have developed devices that transfer print and other media to computer disk or tape. These scanners may be too expensive for your company to purchase at this time, but you may be able to rent them at a fair price. With the advent of facsimile machine technology, text scanning and encoding/decoding over telephone lines will become less expensive. By placing your qualitative data on tape or disk, you preserve it in a small package and can manipulate and analyze it with computer programs later. In the long run, this will often prove cost-effective, especially if you conduct qualitative studies often.

The main thing you should do with qualitative data is search for pattern. This overlaps with the analysis stage, but here we refer to discovering patterns that you can categorize and make sense of later. Select two judges to find patterns in open-end answers. They should look for key ideas, words, and synonyms for those words. They should review about 20 percent of the sample. They can use a content analysis computer subroutine to aid them. The subroutine will search for and list key words from the text the scanner put into the computer. Note that text can be entered into a computer by a human transcriber should a machine scanner prove inadequate or too expensive. Eventually, key words or ideas will emerge; these can then be grouped and later coded for numerical analysis or subjective interpretation. Remember, coded words must represent meanings in context. Isolated words without contextual meaning are less useful.

No matter how you edit qualitative information, do it systematically. I present ten steps to analyze quantitative data in the next section. Review these to see how many of these steps can be incorporated into a review of qualitative data fitness.

Editing Quantitative Data

I spent three years of graduate school as a data analyst. After dealing with dozens of studies, some well done, others haphazard, I developed a good editing system. It consists of these ten steps. I recommend that you or your researcher follow these to ensure quality data. It would be a shame to conduct a flawless study only to junk it at the editing and analysis stage. Remember, garbage in, garbage out.

1. Make a codebook.
2. Review questionnaires/observation forms for errors before data entry.
3. Enter data into the computer.
4. Print a list of data in the computer.
5. Visually examine data list for errors and correct them.
6. Subject data to descriptive analysis.
7. Examine descriptive output for errors and normality.
8. Dump, transform, or fix bad or missing data.
9. Subject data to reliability analysis.
10. Fix or live with reliability errors.

Your particular project may not need this detailed of an editing procedure. Adjust to what fits your needs best. I now explain some of these steps in more detail, so you will fully understand the nature and importance of good editing. Careful editing of data will allow the analyst to prey over the data, to really get a feel for it. Too many statisticians quickly pour the data into the computer, jump to hyperspace, and spew out contingency tables, product space maps, and multiple regression equations. In their zeal, they may miss important information lurking in the data. This can be dangerous and expensive. Good editing will save confusion, misinterpretation, and money in the long run. Many marketing research texts and most statistics books skimp on editing procedure. Preying over your data is so important that I will discuss the ten editing steps in more detail.

The first step directs you (or your analyst) to construct a codebook. This is a matrix of respondent observations in the rows and independent and dependent variables in the columns. Most computerized statistical subroutines accept 80 columns of data and as many rows as the computer has memory space. That is, your computer may permit room for only 800 rows, or 8,000. The codebook should match your questionnaire or observation form exactly. Typically, a codebook will reserve the first two or three columns for respondent identification numbers, then devote as many columns as necessary for independent variables, and dedicate remaining columns for dependent variables. As a general rule, leave no column spaces between variables, as this wastes space, takes more time, and promotes data entry error.

Step two entails scoping each questionnaire/observation form for error. This means you must visually inspect each questionnaire (even machine-scanned forms) for omissions, wild scores (out of range), incompleteness, inconsistencies, ambiguity, and sabotage. Bad questionnaires may have to be discarded. Instruct respondents or proctors to fill in everything on a questionnaire or observation form. Include a category for "no response." That way you won't be in a quandary if data are missing. If a response is missing, you know something is wrong. If you find inconsistencies, illegible responses, or omissions, the best thing to do is contact the respondent or proctor and straighten things out. If this is not feasible, enter a "no response" code into the computer for that respondent, or throw it out. When we mentioned "mortality" in the experimentation chapter, we referred to subjects dropping out of the study on their own, but sometimes you will lose more subjects while editing. This is why I recommend using a few more people than you minimally need. For dependent variables, you have other alternatives in addition to throwing out that case. These are explained below.

Step three is simple. Enter the data into the computer. Train your data entry operators so they don't mess it up. There are some data entry programs available to make this job easier. SPSS offers one such program for mainframes and personal computers; it is called SPSSRAW. There is one thing you must instruct your data entry operators to do: save the data file every ten responses or so. As an undergraduate student several years ago, I entered 1,400 lines of raw data into a computer. The computer went down for a few minutes; I lost everything. After that experience I wrote a subroutine that automatically saved everthing after five lines, no matter what.

After the data are entered, print a hard copy. Then visually examine it to get a feel for the data. Many times I have run down a column of 900 responses and could accurately guess the mean score. It is good to get close to your data. By inspecting the hard copy, you can see major problems such as a whole column of data being out of place. If you notice problems, fix them right then and print another hard copy. Keep doing this until the data set looks right.

Step six asks you to program descriptive statistics for all your data. This is quick and provides a lot of information about range of responses and other details you might want to know. Here is what should be included in the output for a ratio variable: frequencies and percentages for all values of the variable; a histogram, which graphically shows how normal the distribution is; and descriptive statistics such as the range, mode, median, mean, 95 percent confidence interval about the mean, standard deviation, and standard error.

Your next step is to look over these figures and again

check for missing values and scores that are out of range. You can see if you have a normal distribution so you can decide if transforming the variable is necessary. By the way, it is generally not a good idea to transform variables if they don't differ too far from normality. The reason is one of interpretation. It is difficult for you (or at least me) to understand the new metric after a variable is transformed. Imagine you decided to transform a variable to bring variances closer to equality. That is, you want to reduce disparity between variances for several groups. Assume that the variances are proportional to the square of the means, so a logarithmic transformation (log X) is used. The transformed data reduces the disparity, but the new figures are not easy to comprehend for the average marketing manager or researcher. It is a bad idea to stray from your original data unless it is imperative.

If you find something wrong with a response on a variable after the descriptive analysis, you may have to discard it, put in the average value for that group, or put in the value you think the respondent or recorder meant. For example, if an interval scaled variable ranges from one to seven and an eight is scored instead, you could reasonably assume that eight was punched accidentally in the data entry process.

In step nine, you want to check for reliability, consistency, and stability of responses. This may involve a reliability test for a set of attitude questions, or you may run a cross-table on a dependent variable by telephone interviewer to determine if proctors obtained similar responses from respondents. If interviewers called respondents from a random sample, then equivalent responses should obtain among interviewers. If there is a significant difference among interviewers, then you may suspect that one or more interviewers erred or fudged. You may wish to adjust your data set to make it more reliable. After you have completed these steps, you are ready to analyze your data.

QUALITATIVE DATA ANALYSIS

Whereas qualitative measures are quick to assemble, their analysis is slow. Data, in respondents' or observers' own words, contain much variety and individualized expression of perceptions and beliefs. This means that interpretation is subjective and that quantification beyond nominal descriptive measures is difficult and usually inappropriate.

With these restrictions in mind, it is still worthwhile to analyze qualitative data as systematically as possible. If you instruct your focus group moderator or depth interviewer to write up the results, you will get little more than a single reporter's view. This may suffice for exploratory research that precedes the real study, but is probably insufficient for a full-blown qualitative study.

As when editing qualitative data, the analyst must look for meaningful patterns. These may be categories of common expressions, or clusters of behavior. The computer can help locate patterns. Also, I recommend assigning two qualified analysts working independently and concurrently (after training) to interpret patterns. This will delimit each's natural subjectivity and establish some degree of reliability. This is somewhat costly, but necessary, because you don't want to bank your whole study on one person's interpretation.

Qualitative data analysts should attempt to graph their findings, and construct tables and matrices whenever feasible. This will give decision makers visual information about data relationships. A good book to help you systematically study and graph media content is Krippendorff's *Content Analysis: an Introduction to Its Methodology* (1980). Another good qualitative analysis book for your company library is *Qualitative Data Analysis: A Sourcebook of New Methods,* by Miles and Huberman (1984). Check these out. To learn more about qualitative analysis techniques, take an ethnographics or qualitative methods course from the sociology, communication, or anthropology departments at your local university.

QUANTITATIVE DATA ANALYSIS

Surprisingly, quantitative data analysis is usually easier and more straightforward than qualitative analysis. Also, there are many more books, articles, and university courses on statistics than on qualitative analysis. In marketing research, quantitative analysis is much more common. Basic statistics are used much more frequently than multivariate statistics in marketing research, although advances in computer programs and hardware make multivariate approaches available to analysts at a low price. Let's discuss important data analysis considerations for common statistics used in marketing research.

Basic Statistics

Pope (1981: 213) says that basic statistics are all you will usually need. I agree. The appropriate basic statistics, performed and interpreted correctly, suffice for most marketing research studies. Basic statistics have several positive points in their favor. First, many marketing managers have taken basic statistics courses and are familiar with these statistics. Second, there are many good computer programs available that will crunch basic statistics numbers for you. Third, basic statistics stay close to the data. The parsimony principle is enacted.

Basic statistics perform three major functions. They describe central tendencies and variance, draw inferences from a sample about the target population, and note if there are significant differences or relationships among independent variable groups.

I recommend reporting pertinent descriptive statistics for all variables of interest from your study (see editing step six). These summary statistics need not be placed in tables in the body of your report, but should be appended. Histograms, bar charts, line charts, pie charts, and other graphs should accompany these statistics to provide a picture for ease of understanding. Histograms, bar charts, and pie charts should include percentages *and* absolute frequencies, so we know the base from which percentages were calculated.

Line charts should use numbers in the horizontal and vertical axes that are understandable and reasonable, so as not to create false impressions. For example, if you chop off the bottom (or zero point) of the vertical axis, the resultant line will show more impact across time. Further, if you want to make an upward trend soar, just lengthen the metric in the vertical axis (and shorten the horizontal metric) and you will obtain dramatic results guaranteed to mislead the reader in the direction you choose. This is bad. To ensure you don't accidentally commit these sins, read the classic *How to Lie with Statistics* (Huff 1954), and the recent *Misused Statistics: Straight Talk for Twisted Numbers,* by Jaffe and Spirer (1987).

Care should also be taken in reporting results from surveys, whether you are reporting means or percentages. For example, some pollsters omit sample size when reporting figures. They might state something about the true percentage residing within plus or minus three percentage points from the obtained percentage. At a 95 percent confidence level for two percentages, your obtained percentage will automatically be plus or minus three points from true percentages (or lower), regardless of variability, if your sample boasts more than 1,000 subjects. So, inform your reader of sample size and its impact on results.

The same advice applies to hypothesis testing. You will always find significant differences or relationships among groups if the sample size is large enough. Here is an example. Suppose you wanted to test males and females on a new intelligence scale you invented. Suppose there were 100 questions and females obtained a mean score of 87, whereas males averaged 71. If you randomly selected 30 females and 30 males, a t test or F test would show clear significant differences at the 95 percent confidence level. You would rightfully conclude that females scored significantly higher than males in this instance. But what if females averaged 87 and males averaged 85 and sample size remained the same? Obviously, there would not be a significant difference between the sexes. However, if the sample were increased to 2,000 females and 2,000 males, a t test would report a significant difference between these scores at the 95 percent confidence level. The results would showcase an artifact of sample size. You would be remiss if you reported these findings as significant.

Another area of reporting that merits discussion is the type of measurement used for data analysis. In our intelligence test example, we could obtain drastically different results if we used different measurements and different hypothesis tests. Say we hypothesized that women were smarter than men. Our results showed that men averaged 77 correct answers on the test, and women averaged 68. If our sample were again 30 males and 30 females, obviously our hypothesis would find no support from these observations. But, if upon further examination of the raw scores, we found that more women "passed" the test (obtained a score of 60 or above), and more men failed the test, we could compress the ratio test scores into nominal pass/fail data and obtain different results. Using pass/fail data, we could construct a contingency table and show that 25 females passed and only 14 males passed. We would find that females performed significantly better than males on this test. So, by compressing powerful score data down to conservative nominal data, we found major differences in performance between the sexes. I advise against reducing ratio or interview data down to nominal just to prove you are right. If you or your analysts compress data down for the sake of simplicity, and doing so does not camouflage true differences, then there is no deceit in this act.

The most commonly used hypothesis tests in marketing research are chi square, t tests, and F tests (these involve nominal and interval or ratio data). Ordinal variables are not used as much in hypothesis testing in marketing research. But ordinal tests such as Somers' d, the sign test, Wilcoxon signed-rank test, Friedman's test, and the Kruskal-Wallis test are commonly used in marketing research hypothesis testing that involves ordinal data. Most basic statistics texts offer clear explanations and examples of these statistics. I recommend statistics texts by Linton and Gallo (1975) and Ferguson (1981) as good examples.

When using chi square to test relationships between two nominal variables, be sure to show the contingency table associated with your hypothesis test so decision makers can see the relationships. Your table should include count, row percentage, column percentage, and total percentage for each cell and margin. If you are not testing hypotheses with nominal data, but are merely showing the degree of association, the contingency coefficient should be reported along with the table.

If your hypothesis tests involve nominally scaled independent variables and interval or ratio scaled dependent variables, you will use t tests or F tests. F tests must be used when there is more than one independent variable or the independent variable has more than two levels. Here is what should be included when reporting results of F tests: the analysis of variance (ANOVA) summary table with banners; group counts, means, standard deviations, standard errors, minimum and maximum scores, and the 95 percent confidence interval for each group's mean; and if there are more than two means, then the results of appropriate multiple comparison tests (such as the Tukey or Duncan tests); the association and effect size (e.g., eta squared, omega squared, Cohen's d) (see Plutchik 1984: 123–132); and power to detect significant differences. If there are significant interactions, these should be plotted and interpreted.

It seems like I am demanding that every little statistical detail be reported—and I am. Little details may save you from a lawsuit. Now, all these details need not be explicated in the text of your report, but should at least be appended. A decision maker needs detailed information and visual representation of findings. Computers can easily spew out all this information in a few seconds at nominal cost, so why skimp? Note, however, I am not suggesting that you pad your report with endless tables and figures that are not germane to hypotheses and research questions. That would be wasteful. I recommend including only necessary but *complete* information. Some marketing researchers delude their clients into thinking that "brief" equates with "concise." Decision makers who get only "selected" bits of information, or worse, who want only the executive summary, will be inclined to make bad decisions.

If research needs call for correlation (such as Pearson product-moment correlation or Spearman's rho) include a scatterplot and a complete correlation matrix. Again, it is not expensive to produce this information, and it may prove worthwhile, especially if a high correlation turns out to be curvilinear (see Kimble 1978: 180–200). If you are correlating several variables, you may find it nigh impossible to make sense of the matrix and the interrelationships among the variables. In this case, you should turn to multivariate techniques such as factor analysis to to get a firmer grasp on your data. Let's now turn to multivariate statistics used in marketing research.

Pros and Cons of Multivariate Statistics

Basic statistics may be used most often in marketing research, and may be parsimonious, but they are not always appropriate. Sometimes a data set will need more complex statistics for adequate analysis. This is where more complex models and multivariate data analysis come in. The benefits of multivariate statistics (usually characterized by three or more interdependent or dependent variables) are many. These include understanding higher order relationships among a group of correlated variables, or reducing these variables into larger factors, or finding a linear combination of variables that together best separate a nominal variable's groups, or plotting product similarity data, or grouping people into clusters, or finding the relative importance of attributes when compared to each other. In other words, the multivariate family of statistics address the complexities of the complex world we live in.

Multivariate techniques are now computer programmed for fast (and I mean fast) computation. If you were to conduct a factor analysis study by hand, it would take you a year to do it and many computational errors would be committed in the process. Modern computers and subroutines can compute a factor analysis instantly, without computational error. And these computer programs are easy to use, and they're available for microcomputers—at a reasonable price. Contrary to popular belief, multivariate statistical programs are inexpensive to purchase and use. Statistical programs are discussed in more detail later.

During the past ten years, the marketing research profession has led the way for all the social sciences in the area of multivariate statistics. The *Journal of Marketing Research* features benchmark articles on clustering techniques, confirmatory factor analysis, nonmetric multidimensional scaling, and structural models with latent variables. There are many examples of these techniques in marketing and consumer behavior journals. Additionally, many proprietary multivariate techniques (e.g., some conjoint analysis techniques) were developed especially for marketing applications.

Additionally, there are a few good applications-oriented multivariate statistics texts (see Aaker 1971; Cooley & Lohnes 1971; and especially Hair et al. 1987; Monge & Cappella 1980). Finally, Sage Publications of Newbury Park, California, have organized a series of some seventy papers dealing with quantitative analysis. Twenty-two of these papers relate to multivariate techniques and applications. All of the papers are inexpensive (about $7.00 each), and deal with complex techniques in a straightforward manner with good examples. There are definitely plenty of recent articles, books, and monographs on multivariate statistics.

Universities, the American Marketing Association, private organizations such as the Burke Institute, and software companies such as SPSS offer courses, seminars, and conferences on multivariate statistics. I recommend that all marketing managers, entrepreneurs, and researchers bone up on multivariate applications. Otherwise, you may be left out in the cold. In today's competitive market, not knowing multivariate statistics is akin to lacking basic microcomputer savvy.

You can see I advocate at least a cursory understanding of multivariate statistics, else you would not have a clue as to if or how they should or should not be used in your marketing studies. Before discussing these techniques, I must issue caveats about multivariate statistics.

First, most multivariate statistics are extremely complex. They require many subjective decisions at various stages of computation. If you make the wrong decision at any point, you could obtain garbage—and not know it. The algorithms are complex. Only a mathematician or statistician would likely have the necessary background to figure out the relevance of the computations. Business students typically learn calculus, basic statistics, and regression, but not complex multivariate statistics. Some graduate marketing research courses devote time to multivariate applications (mine does), but there is no time to provide the detail necessary for you to master these statistics; just acquiring proficiency is a major undertaking. Usually, a brief introduction is all you can expect to get in a graduate marketing research course or a professional seminar.

For you to obtain a cursory understanding of the inner workings of these techniques, you would need to take courses devoted to the study of each method—and read a lot on your own. This would take years. Meanwhile, new and better techniques are lurking on the fringe, threatening to topple the techniques you struggled to comprehend. I remember how knowledgeable I felt after completing a course in factor analysis. Two years later I was forced to take confirmatory factor analysis seminars just to barely keep pace. All I can say is plunge in with your eyes open.

Tips for Multivariate Statistics

Before discussing specific techniques, here are a few general tips that may help you. Don't become enamored with multivariate statistics just because they are elegant. Don't fit the research problem to the technique; do the opposite. Don't rely on multivariate statistics to fix a bad study; it will only make it worse. Don't buffalo others with multivariate statistics; ensure that you and your researchers clearly communicate findings to decision makers. Append ancillary graphs; place only key tables and figures in the text. Make sure you obtain an adequate sample size (current opinion sets a minimum n of 100). Ensure that you correctly use the appropriate techniques to adequately address information needs.

You should determine which multivariate statistics you intend to use during the data analysis planning stage so you can set up questionnaires, obervation forms, and their item scales accordingly. Then plan which computer programs work best for the type of analysis you require. When selecting multivariate statistics for your needs, obtain a copy of *A Guide for Selecting Statistical Techniques for Analyzing Social Science Data* by Andrews et al. (1981). This guide features a complete decision tree for most statistics.

When determining which multivariate techniques to use for your study, it helps to break down techniques in a decision tree format. First ask if you need dependence or interdependence methods. Dependence methods consist of independent and dependent variables (these can be further broken down into how many dependent and independent variables you have). Interdependence methods make no distinction between dependent and independent variables; all variables are analyzed together.

Once you have decided on the dependence or interdependence family, determine if you want metric (equal intervals between numbers) or nonmetric measurement of your variables. Finally, determine which variables you want to analyze, and choose the proper technique and statistical program.

Dependence Techniques

There are five major types of dependence techniques: multiple correlation and regression, multivariate analysis of variance and covariance, multiple discriminant analysis, canonical analysis, and conjoint analysis. Of these, multiple regression is by far the most used technique in marketing research and business in general. Most marketers with business degrees have been exposed to regression analysis either in statistics courses, operations research, marketing research, or forecasting. Because regression is used to predict in marketing (e.g., sales), I recommend that you stay familiar with regression techniques and applications. Lewis-Beck (1980) and Achen (1982) have each prepared a concise, inexpensive monograph on regression applications and interpretation. Most statistics texts do a good job explaining regression.

Nowadays, there is a regression family technique for just about every regression contingency. If you discover a curvilinear relationship, you can use polynomial regression. If some of your predictor variables are nominal, you can use dummy variable regression or multiple classification analysis (MCA). Multiple regression produces one predictor equation describing the relationship between predictor variables and a dependent variable. If you want to look at interactions instead, choose automatic interaction detector (AID), which produces a tree of two-way splits based upon the independent variable that accounts for the most dependent variable variation (see Aaker and Day 1982: 565–573). If you want to do multiple regression but there are intervening or latent variables to contend with, check out path analysis or structural models with latent variables.

If there is more than one dependent variable and more than one independent variable, then perform canonical correlation, the true multivariate extension of multiple regression, where two sets of interval data are used. Canonical analysis, by combining dependent variables, saves the researchers from running separate regressions on each dependent variable. A composite dependent variable is produced instead. Hair et al. (1987: 187–231) and Thompson (1984) provide good description and applications of canonical analysis as a multivariate predictor model. Tucker and Chase (1980: 205–228) do an excellent job of describing the canonical correlation model and discuss its use as an interdependence technique to measure association between two sets of dependent variables. Canonical correlation is being used more often in marketing research than in the past. Some statisticians advise using canonical analysis only as a last-ditch technique. They consider it too ambiguous. I disagree. The pitfalls of canonical analysis exist, but all multivariate techniques require subjective judgment. As in all risky business endeavors, exercise caution and restraint, but don't turn away from a good technique such as canonical analysis.

If you have more than one dependent, intervally scaled variable and one or more nominally scaled independent variables, consider multiple analysis of variance (MANOVA), in which a correlated set of dependent variables separates independent variable groups. If any of the dependent variables significantly separated an independent variable's groups, then univariate comparison tests could be used to find which groups significantly differ from each other. In essence, MANOVA saves computations; you need not perform separate ANOVAs on each dependent variable.

If you have more than five dependent variables in your set, consider multiple discriminant analysis (MDA). MDA is similar to MANOVA, but the correlated dependent variables in the set act in concert to separate groups of the independent variable. The dependent variables with the highest loadings are used to label the factor (discriminant function) and its centroids (multivariate means). Note that in MDA, independent and dependent terms are reversed. So normal dependent variables are called predictors, and they separate nominally scaled criterion groups. MDA is a popular technique among marketing researchers and is definitely worth learning. MDA could be used to find which demographic and psychographic variables best separate groups (say, users versus nonusers of a product). This is an adequate way to identify and explain differences between these two groups.

In recent years, the rising star among multivariate dependence techniques in marketing is conjoint analysis. In conjoint measurement, the dependent variable is ordinal, and independent variables are nominal. Conjoint analysis is used in product development. The product is described with a list of attributes, and respondents trade off attributes or make a judgment of a full profile of attributes. The end result is relative utility values for each level of an attribute.

To my knowledge, major statistical packages such as BMDP, SAS, and SPSS do not yet offer conjoint analysis software. However, there are dedicated conjoint programs available if you search (e.g., Sawtooth Software's Adaptive Conjoint Analysis [ACA] System). We will see increasingly more software support for conjoint analysis in the near future as this technique catches on.

Interdependence Techniques

There are three families of interdependence techniques: factor analysis, multidimensional scaling, and cluster analysis. According to Aaker and Day (1983: 537), these statistical families are interdependent "because they analyze the interdependence between questions, variables, or objects." All three techniques are used often in marketing research settings.

Factor analysis methods analyze interrelationships among variables to find underlying theoretical dimensions, or in market research to reduce a set of metric variables to a few explanatory factors. In marketing, we use factor analysis to obtain the most parsimonious explanation of several variables (say key product attributes), and use the reduced data set for subsequent analyses. Factor analysis, like all multivariate techniques, requires several levels of decision making, such as choosing correlation or covariance matrices, or rotating factors orthogonally or obliquely. With the current emphasis on confirming everything (factor analysis is historically considered exploratory), new factor analysis techniques have been developed that not only explore relationships, but simultaneously compare patterns, say of users versus nonusers of a product. This latter type of factor analysis is becoming well known in marketing and is called confirmatory factor analysis. For a good introduction to confirmatory factor analysis, read J. S. Long's (1983) monograph on the subject. For a clear introduction of factor analysis in general, read Kim and Mueller (1978a; 1978b) and Tucker et al. (1981: 199–202).

Multidimensional scaling (MDS) is often used in marketing research and has been increasing in popularity over the past ten years. Basically, MDS provides a perceptual space map of respondents' judgments of preference or similarity. By viewing the map, we can see products plotted in space near axes. Products that are perceived as similar or receive similar rankings will be closer together in joint space. Ideal products can also be added in and existing products can be compared visually with these ideals. This gives marketers an idea of how their products are perceived compared to others and to consumers' ideal product. The Kruskal and Wish (1978) monograph describes MDS quite clearly.

A technique that also allows for visual mapping is cluster analysis. You can view scatter diagrams of cluster observations, dendograms, and cluster line charts. In cluster analysis, the goal is to classify objects (e.g., people) according to natural relationships. Objects are clustered based on their distance or similarity gathered from ratings on certain variables. The primary use of cluster analysis in marketing is to segment markets. Again, like all multivariate techniques, clustering requires the researcher to make several subjective judgments, so a sound knowledge of this common technique used in marketing is needed. For a good general discussion of cluster analysis, purchase the monograph by Aldenderfer and Blashfield (1984). For cluster analysis applications in marketing research and a rundown on cluster analysis software, read Punj and Stewart (1983). Since cluster analysis has become so popular, some companies have devoted themselves to producing complete cluster analysis services (e.g., Claritas features a cluster system called PRIZM/UPDATE that reflects neighborhood behavior profiles).

As you can see from the variety of multivariate techniques, there is a lot to know about these complex methods. In addition to the tips and resources presented here, you need to get hands-on experience using these techniques to obtain a sufficient grasp of their value and use in marketing contexts. Very few researchers and statisticians can competently use many of these techniques. I know I cannot. But we must struggle along. We can never learn a complex technique without experimenting with it. Obtain the software for these techniques and play with some published data sets; this will help you understand the multivariate models. Let's turn now to examine some of the software available.

COMPUTER SOFTWARE FOR RESEARCH
AND STATISTICS

Over the past twenty years, we have seen the statistical software market go from one mainframe package (BMD in 1961) to a wide array of inexpensive and powerful programs for microcomputers that are available today. The advent of affordable software and microcomputers with ample memory means that marketing managers and researchers can afford to analyze data in-house. There is no need to farm out the data analysis for a few thousand dollars. Assuming your business owns powerful microcomputers, you can purchase all the statistical software you will need for the cost of one data analysis done outside your company.

There is nothing but good news down the line for statistical software. During the next few years, competition will bring more good software into the market and reduce prices. It pays to keep your eyes open for good deals. No doubt many statistical packages will not suit your needs, so be a wise shopper. Pay attention to articles that compare software. We now review some classic and recent statistical packages.

Classic Statistical Software

Beginning in the late 1960s and progressing through the 1970s, there has been a steady increase of comprehensive statistical packages for mainframe computers (such as the IBM 370 and Cyber 70). We examine these major packages and their primary uses. If you have access to these, you may wish to perform some statistics with one package, and other statistics with another.

The first and still one of the best is the BMD series of computer programs. The BMD (Biomedical Computer Programs) package with the most longevity is the BMDP series (Dixon 1975). BMDP features most of the univariate and bivariate statistics you would likely need, and is especially strong in ANOVA programs. BMDP is pretty good at data sorting and editing. Regarding multivariate programs, BMDP has always been a good bet for canonical analysis and cluster analysis. BMDP multivariate programs have been thoroughly debugged over the years. You cannot go wrong with BMDP. It does have problems, however. The manual is a bore, designed more for computer programmers than data analysts. Until you become accustomed to it, BMDP is not easy to use, largely because numbers and symbols are used instead of familiar words. For example, the canonical correlation subroutine is entitled "BMDP6M." The SPSS program is called "CANCORR." Which will you remember? However, setting up BMDP programs is very simple—once you get used to it.

BMDP now offers a personal computer version called BMDP/PC. According to Fridlund (1986), the documentation and online performance equates with the mainframe version. In other words, the package is not user friendly. Its graphics capabilities are limited. All things considered, though, I recommend it.

OSIRIS III (1973) is a sophisticated group of programs developed at the University of Michigan. Its primary feature is data editing, sorting, organizing. OSIRIS used to feature multivariate programs that other packages did not, such as MDS, but other companies such as SAS have these now. To my knowledge, the OSIRIS people have not developed their statistical software for personal computers.

The Statistical Packages for the Social Sciences (SPSS, Nie et al. 1975) is the most commonly used statistics software series. It is the package I use the most. It is written in FORTRAN, and the fixed input format statement looks just like a typical FORTRAN statement. I find this satisfactory since I know FORTRAN, but others find it cumbersome. The SPSS manual and updates are clear, concise, and informative. In my opinion, SPSS has the best documentation around. Writing programs using SPSS is not difficult, since key words resemble natural language (e.g., INPUT FORMAT, FACTOR). SPSS features good descriptive and basic inferential statistics. They have good correlation, regression, discriminant analysis, and especially factor analysis programs. Over the years, they have augmented their extensive statistics mix with Joreskog's confirmatory factor analysis, reliability analysis, MANOVA, cluster analysis, and hierarchical log-linear models. SPSS has always been weak in time series analysis, but has recently introduced a time series/forecasting/ ARIMA series of subroutines called Trends.

SPSS also has an excellent microcomputer version available, which includes many of their mainframe features. SPSS used to be weak in graphics, but now features a strong pc graphics portfolio. Their SPSS/PC+ reads Lotus and dBASE files, and has a nice Microsoft graphics capability called Chart. The basic cost for the pc system is about $800. If you desire special features and new statistics, add about $300 each. All in all—it's a best buy. You will get your money's worth.

For your regression and analysis of variance needs, check out the venerated Statistical Analysis System (SAS, Barr et al., 1976). SAS has long been noted for graphics and good multivariate programs such as cluster analysis and recently, MDS. These programs require a bit of work on the mainframe, but you will get good results.

If you like the mainframe SAS, you will like PC SAS, the microcomputer version. Like its mainframe cousin, PC SAS can crunch mountains of data, assuming your personal computer has memory space for it. I predict that by the early 1990s almost all commercially available personal computers will have the capacity to store acres of data and have plenty of memory left over for multivariate computations. If you conduct extremely large surveys, then PC SAS is for you. It's ready now for the microcomputers of the future. PC SAS is interactive and user friendly (except for documentation). It costs $1,500 for a year's use for the basic program. If you conduct studies with large data sets and need a variety of statistics, PC SAS is the right choice.

The statistical packages just described comprise the bulk of classic statistical software that you can still buy today. There are many other classic software packages that have survived the test of time and are still available. Many of these are suited for one family of statistics or are dedicated to one technique. Some are in the public domain (see

Cooley & Lohnes 1971 for several examples of multivariate programs). Others are available commercially. One of the most sought after independent software packages is the Joreskog and Sorbom (1983) LISREL VI program for confirmatory factor analysis and structural equation models. The manual is difficult to follow, even though it represents a vast improvement in readability over past versions. The LISREL statistical packages may still have bugs; test yours thoroughly before using it for a real project.

Recent Statistical Software

Recently, new statistical software packages have emerged that rival BMDP, SPSS, and SAS for the microcomputer research user market. These merit review. The Anderson-Bell company has two packages available, ABSTAT and ABTAB, both inexpensive. ABSTAT features a basic graphics package, common descriptive and inferential statistics, cross-tabulation, Lotus and dBASE file importing, plus report functions. ABSTAT is interactive, easy to use, and relatively fast. According to Minno (1985: 62), "ABTAB is one of the most complete cross-tabulation packages that I have seen." Check these packages out.

Another software package worth considering is NWA Statpak. It features several good regression programs, including polynomial regression. Whereas all the microcomputer statistical programs I have mentioned are designed for IBM PC (XT or AT usually), NWA Statpak also works on a Macintosh. If you need to do regression and don't sample too many subjects (this package is limited in memory), NWA Statpak is for you. Also, it is inexpensive.

If you want to combine statistics with great graphics, seek Statgraphics. The package features good descriptive statistics, time series analysis, even canonical correlation. Other Statgraphics highlights for marketing researchers is its sampling plan and size utility and experimental design subroutine. The programs run on AT&T and Tandy computers, in addition to IBM. This package is also inexpensive.

The microcomputer statistics package I am most impressed with is Systat. Fridlund (1986) concurs. It performs the most statistics, including nonlinear regression and MDS. It is fast. It works on a variety of microcomputers. Once you get used to it, you can program quickly. Documentation is adequate. Graphics are okay. At $600, it is dirt cheap for what you get. I recommend purchasing Systat no matter what other packages you buy.

There are many other good personal computer software packages on the market today. CRUNCH is good. True to its name, it crunches lots of numbers. It performs standard statistics, reliability analysis, and complex transformations. And it is inexpensive. There are other packages worth checking out that are also inexpensive. These include Microtab, Surveytab, Synthesis, and Spring-Stat.

Doubtless, there are many more good statistical packages for microcomputers. Some are too expensive. I have presented some of the packages I am familiar with that I believe present cost-effective value. But you should not rely on my word for what is good. *Marketing News* lists all the latest statistical programs in their software directory— and sometimes reviews packages (e.g., Minno 1985). Other periodicals, such as *Computer Intelligence, InfoWorld,* and *PC WORLD,* conduct studies and reviews of software. As a value-driven consumer, you should take it upon yourself to check these packages out. Many manufacturers offer trial periods or demonstration disks.

A few tips: don't automatically assume that packages will work the way manufacturers claim they will, regardless of the firm's reputation for quality. Always check the fidelity of each statistical subroutine you wish to use by running data with known parameters. Ensure that the company services what it sells. Check to see if their telephone service center meets your needs. If you work in a large company, you may be able to obtain substantial discounts when buying several programs.

Microcomputer analysis of macrodata is the near future for marketing research. There is already a myriad of marketing and marketing research related software available with more being introduced every year. I counted thirty-three new marketing applications software packages in the Software Directory Update in the November 6, 1987 issue of *Marketing News,* and found fifteen more in the January 4, 1988 issue. Your company will gain a competitive edge—cost-effectively—by taking advantage of what is available now.

8

Reporting Results

The study has been planned. executed, and analyzed. What is the end result, the product? The product is words, either written or spoken. The product is information, not data. Data were collected; information is given. Some researchers give their clients a stack of tables and statistics and say, in effect, "Weed through this." The client gratefully accepts the pile of "information," wades through the executive summary, and then shelves it. That's not cost-effective research.

As a client you should expect a clear, concise, correctly written report from the researcher. You should also expect an oral explanation of any and all aspects of the report. In this chapter, you learn the proper components of written and oral reports. We also discuss ethics, then how you can benefit from cost-effective research now and in the future.

WRITING THE REPORT

A good report consists of several ingredients: it looks good, it's well organized, it is complete, and it contains recommendations. Helpful appendices are included. And it is clearly written. Let's discuss each of these so you will know a good one when you see one and can write an effective report yourself.

Appearance Counts

For any product to sell, it must be packaged correctly to attract favorable attention from consumers. This axiom holds for written research reports. As a research consumer, you expect the report to look official, authoritative, flawless, even beautiful. The binding need not be expensive, but it should look conservative. This means it should be black, dark blue, maroon, or gray, not pink. The paper should be a heavy cotton white bond. If you are a professional researcher, or are a marketing manager preparing a research paper, you may need to use standard company binders and paper. Otherwise, keep it simple (remember the parsimony principle?) and powerful.

The type font should be dark, crisp, and a bit oversized (ten-pitch). I strongly recommend you use a desktop publishing system and a laser printer to prepare and print your document. If your company cannot afford these things yet, buy time on your local photocopy shop's equipment. If you know what you are doing, you'll find this quite inexpensive.

Make your graphics crisp, informative, and interesting. Use your statistical program and your microcomputer to construct graphs. Place ancillary graphs in an appendix. This will add several pages to the report, giving it "poundage" quality, and will not detract from the report proper.

Like a new car, if your report looks good, the customer will get immediate satisfaction. However, this satisfaction will quickly wane if the report lacks substance.

Follow the Proper Format

Proper report format ranges from a memo to a very formal work complete with transmittal letters, cover pages, and the like. If a short research project was done in-house, a memorandum may suffice. If the project is major, the report should be completed in a formal manner. Unless a "request for proposal" mandates a particular structure, a typical format for a business report should contain these elements:

1. front title page
2. transmittal letter
3. inside title page
4. table of contents
5. executive summary
   a. objectives
   b. principal methods
   c. key findings/limitations
   d. primary conclusions/recommendations
6. body of the report
   a. introduction
   b. methods
   c. results
   d. conclusions/recommendations
7. appendices

Let's discuss these components in more detail. The first three parts are simple and optional. You must include a title page, but you need not have two of them. The front title is printed in BIG letters and grabs the reader's attention. The inside title page is normal size and includes all the relevant details such as for whom the report is intended and who conducted the research, the date, and, of course, the title. Use a descriptive title, not generic. Don't put "KAYAK STUDY"; put "KAYAK MARKET SEGMENTATION PROFILE." The transmittal letter is optional but recommended. It is simply a letter from the researcher to the client stating something like "Here is the report. . . We'll give the oral presentation next Tuesday. . . If you have questions, please call." the transmittal is a nice gesture and serves the dual purpose of a packing slip and a contract.

The table of contents follows. Set up the table of contents based upon headings and subheadings in the report. Always include page numbers. Sometimes it helps to also include a table of "tables and figures" if the report contains several of these.

Without a doubt, the executive summary, or synopsis, abstract, is the part of the report most often read by decision makers. Needless to say, it must be good. The executive summary should be as clear and concise as you can make it. State the study purpose, the prime objective, in a single sentence. State the principal method used in one line. State key findings and compelling limitations in one to seven lines. Conclude in one line; recommend imperative actions. If you do this, it will be read in its entirety. I guarantee it.

The body of the report expands the executive summary. The report proper is complete, not just concise. In general, follow the same format as the executive summary, but don't skimp on important details. Believe me, smart executives who intend to act on the research recommendations will take the time to study the report. But make it easy for readers to find what they're looking for. Use headings and subheadings. Itemize; place important figures in the text.

In the introduction, state the problem/opportunity. List objectives and key information needs. Provide necessary background, summarize and apply previous research, define key terms, state the scope of the project. Make hypotheses and pose research questions. Provide a flow chart of the study.

In the methods section concisely describe everything. Pay particular attention to operationalizing independent and dependent variables. Discuss sampling procedures and population characteristics. Adequately describe methods used and the data analysis plan.

The results comprise the heart of the report. Start by addressing key hypothesis tests and research questions. Get right to the principal information. Include all directly relevant statistics, tables, and figures. Tables and figures must be mentioned before the reader sees them. They must be explained and discussed (else append them). Tables and figures must be properly labeled. Include a limitations section, where rival hypotheses are stated, weaknesses noted, and warnings made.

Summarize briefly after each major section, or in the conclusions section. After summarizing, draw conclusions about the findings that will objectively (as possible) persuade the reader as to the real world significance of findings. Make recommendations, but stick to the data. Don't extrapolate beyond what you would feel comfortable making a deposition about in court. Recommendations are necessary, even if management doesn't want to hear them. A medical doctor recommends certain treatments for ailments, correct? Stand by your study, and let the decision maker decide what to do. You merely advise based upon your findings, which represent a small but important piece of the decision pie. If you don't advise, what are they paying you for?

Another major part of the report is the appendix section. You should include as many appendices as are needed to provide relevant but rather detailed information that is not essential to the body of the report. The first appendix is the bibliography. The second set of appendices contains information from the introduction and methods sections, such as pertinent tables or figures from secondary sources, or copies of questionnaires and field procedures. Detailed information regarding sampling and pilot testing would be included here. The third set makes up the bulk of appendices. Here we place additional graphs and tables from the results. If you follow this advice, your report will be well structured and complete. Now all you need do is write it clearly.

Get the Message Across

To write clearly, serve the interests of your reader. This means your writing should be more than clear, concise, and correct, it should also be creative and convincing. This means avoid technical jargon that is unfamiliar to your audience, but find unique ways to bridge the gap between technical information and your reader. Make the complex simple. Remember to interpret methods and findings.

Use numbers, words, and visuals to get the meaning across. Use numbers, for they are truly the universal language. Numbers remain the same across cultures. Everyone is particularly drawn to percentages; use these whenever possible. Use words to describe, explain, and convince. With words, you can quote, provide examples, state opinions, relate experiences, compare and contrast. Words help make sense of numbers and visual aids. Use visual aids such as models, flow charts, line charts, histograms, scatterplots, perceptual maps, and pie charts. A pie chart combines numbers and words in a visual setting. Use pictographs. Include photographs and illustrations, if they would save a thousand words. Use cross-tables, lists, and columns of numbers. Visual presentation of information is inherently interesting. Almost everything is visually oriented. Serve your client by combining numbers, words, and visual aids whenever possible.

Obtaining Communication Skills

Report writing demands a set of skills that match those required to conduct the research. So, assign report writing to people who are good technical writers. If you are the person responsible for compiling and writing research reports, take writing courses at a local university. The courses to take include business communication or business writing, technical writing, and journalistic writing. These three courses will teach you, respectively, how to write in proper business format, how to prepare technical reports, and how to write quickly and clearly. If taking university courses will inconvenience you, consider taking a business writing or report writing seminar.

If you don't have time to do either of these, I suggest you purchase a writing handbook that emphasizes business and research writing (see Hodges & Whitten 1986). Also, there are several good business communication texts available today. I recommend that you acquire one of these fine books for your library (see Lesikar 1983; Majors [in press]; Murphy & Pick 1980; Sigband & Bateman 1985; and Treece 1980). These books discuss research report writing and also feature business and professional public speaking, our next subject.

ORAL PRESENTATION

Oral presentation of written findings may not be necessary, especially for simple reports, but it often contributes to a better understanding of the results. Here I discuss oral presentation format for research findings. These tips will help you recognize a good oral presentation when you see and hear one, and prepare you to do a good job when you give one. There are several things to do when planning and delivering research results. Prepare your audience, materials, and self. Rehearse. Set a time limit. Deliver competently and confidently. Use visual aids. Answer questions. Conclude. Let's discuss these important aspects of presenting research orally.

Plan and Prepare

What you do before you speak will determine the success of your presentation. First, prepare your audience. Find out who will be there and where the presentation will be given. Determine what they expect of you (ask). Confirm the speaking engagement, even if you are speaking to just one person. Ideally, you should address key decision makers and their advisors. So, if you were discussing the results of a product comparison test, representatives from marketing, finance, research and development, and production should all be present. Ensure that they all have copies of the report long before your presentation. Ask them to read it and prepare questions before they arrive.

Next, get yourself and your materials together. Thoroughly familiarize yourself with all aspects of the study. Be ready to field any question. Plan your speech and what you must cover. Outline it and prepare simple cue notes with key words inscribed. Get your supporting materials together. This includes your notes, raw data (maybe they want to look at it), and visual aids.

You can use the same visual aids in your presentation that were in the report, but don't use complex tables (rows and columns of numbers bore people), unless you have highlighted bottom line figures. Use figures that dramatically emphasize your points. Pie charts, line charts, and histograms work well. Use photos, physical models, and handouts.

Decide on how you will present visual aids. For small groups, chalkboards and flip charts work. Transparencies work for all audience sizes, but remember that people tend to fall asleep as soon as a projector is activated. Slides work best for large audiences. Many companies specialize in preparing slides for business presentations. Check these out. Handouts are good, except that the audience tends to focus on the handout instead of you.

When using visual aids in speeches, remember these tips. The visual aid must be easily seen. That is, make it large and clear, use bright colors, and keep it simple. The visual aid must contribute to your talk. Never use visual aids to fill in time or divert attention away from you. Never wholly depend upon visual aids, as something invariably goes wrong in the middle of your presentation. The projector light bulb burns out, the flip chart falls to the floor, the chalk breaks, and the slides jam. Arrange for visual aid equipment and triple check to make sure everything is satisfactory.

As a great football player once said: "Practice, practice, practice." Practice your speech, practice working with the visual aids, practice answering likely questions. If you rehearse you will get the bugs out and do a good job. Rehearsing is like pilot testing—it is an integral step in delivering a professional presentation.

When you rehearse, you will practice timing. By timing, I mean you will hone down your speech to fit into the time limit. How long should a research presentation take? A half hour at most. Figure it will take five to fifteen minutes to deliver your speech, five to fifteen minutes to field questions, and one minute to conclude. Organize your speech into segments, and rehearse each one. These segments correspond to the written report format. The speech features an introduction, a body, and a conclusion. Let's examine how these are optimally incorporated into the speech.

Stand and Deliver

Here are suggestions to make your speech informative and persuasive. First, during the introduction, open with a statement about the opportunity or problem. If you were reporting on the kayak comparison test, you might begin your presentation with "Whose kayak is best, ours or theirs?" Or you might start with "You asked me to find out which kayak consumers prefer to use on the water... I found out." Or, "Our research shows you need to change three things on your kayak to beat the competition."

Spend time developing the need. Make your client glad you supplied the organization with this information. Spend a short amount of time on method. Just present the high-lights. Refer them to the report for more details. Show a flowchart of the operations involved in the study. Devote most of your time to the results, but don't provide every detail. Again, refer them to the report. Present principal findings and support them with key bits of evidence. Add impact to the findings by emphasizing a couple of visual aids that dramatically highlight important observations.

When using a visual aid, point to it as you speak. High-light the important parts of the aid. Get rid of it as soon as you finish with it so your audience retains their focus on you. Exclude visual aids that do not directly contribute to the talk.

When concluding, summarize and interpret key find-ings, then recommend action. Do not go beyond what was written in the report. After you have stated your recom-mendations, open the floor for questions. Answer their queries and challenges to the best of your ability. Do not hedge. Speak clearly in common terms. If you don't know an answer, say so, then add that you will find out (if you can). Do not apologize for the report. Refer them to the limitations section. Watch your clock to ensure you keep to the time schedule. Be polite. Serve your customer. When the question and answer period ends, conclude again and re-emphasize key recommendations.

It's okay to persuade. Do more than provide information. Omit unimportant data and showcase important information. Don't deceive; do persuade. Be objective and provide evidence to support your expert opinion.

Here are a few delivery tips to make your presentation top-notch. Choose words carefully so your audience will receive the message you intended. Use your voice. Vary your pitch, rate, volume, and tone to keep things interesting. Nothing is more boring than a quiet, slow monotone. Use your eyes to maintain contact with each individual in the audience. Ignore bad advice such as "Look at their foreheads" or "Pick one nice person out and speak to her." Slowly scan back and forth to include everyone in your gaze. Your eyes are the most expressive part of your body. Use them to emphasize key points and to keep tabs on the attention level of your audience. Act like you are conversing with friends on a topic of mutual interest. Look at your audience; you are conversing with them.

Let's talk about physical appearance and body language. Wear clothing appropriate to the occasion and your position as an authority on the topic. Stand up straight and keep your knees slightly bent and your hands in front of you. Act as if you are an athlete ready to compete. Picture a baseball or tennis player. They stand in a readiness posture when performing. So should you. If you slouch, cross your legs, lean on a lectern, bury your hands in your pockets, or obliquely face the audience, you lose effect. Use natural gestures and move around; use your surroundings. Natural movement will relax you and permit you to think on your feet. However, don't nervously pace or wring your hands. This distracts your audience and dissipates the impact of your speech.

If you thoroughly know your subject and feel a genuine interest in it; if you practice, practice, practice; and focus on the topic and audience, rather than on your ner-vousness—you will speak competently and confidently. You can increase your public-speaking confidence by en-rolling in a university course in speech or business commu-nication, taking a seminar such as a Dale Carnegie work-shop, or joining a Toastmasters club. By delivering research results competently, you increase the value of the study to your client and organization.

ETHICAL CONSIDERATIONS

I have scattered references to ethics throughout the book, but I feel it is necessary to bring it up again. Accord-ing to Hendon (1986), marketing is so competitive that it's like a battlefield out there. Philip Kotler, a well-respected marketing professor, teamed up with Ravi Singh to write an article entitled "Marketing Warfare in the 1980s" (1981). The samurai battle philosophy is popular in mar-keting and business. Everyone is quoting Musashi, Sun Tzu, Clausewitz, and Machiavelli. The analogies are fun, but there is a major difference: war kills; marketing serves. Some companies forget that they and their competitors are striving to *serve* their customers the best they can. More emphasis is spent on competing than on contributing. Gaining marketing share becomes more important than meeting customers' needs. Many companies have taken to comparative advertising in which they disparage com-petitors' products. Aspirin and eye drops have been taint-ed. Unfriendly takeovers are on the rise. Some companies have sold sensitive technology to enemy countries. Cartels fix prices. Investors engage in insider trading. And the list goes on. Fair competition is healthy. This country has been built on the principle of fair competition. Marketing research, like marketing itself, is an important part of a company's strength.

Marketing researchers and the companies who use information obtained through research must be responsible and ethical, not merely "legal." If you have to ask your corporate lawyer if it's okay to promote and sell your product under the guise of research, you are considering ethics, not just legalities. If you engage in research activity that is unlawful, you will go to jail and your company will lose a lot of money. That research is not cost-effective. If you get caught conducting research that *may* be unethical, your company's reputation will suffer. And that research is not cost-effective. Here are my thoughts about certain aspects of ethics and marketing research.

Espionage

It is permissable, even necessary, to find out all you reasonably can about your competitors. It is okay to buy their products and dissemble them. General Motors devotes a lot of floor space to stripped-down cars built by their competitors. Tsunami Products regularly tests our kayaks against our competitors' in a variety of settings. We tear apart their rudder assemblies and figure out ways of making ours better and cheaper. But we do not copy their designs and techniques. It is not okay to steal ideas from others.

It is ethical to thoroughly research secondary sources to obtain information on your competitors. We do this all the time. We read all publications that compare products. We use DIALOG information services to check out our competitor's trademarks. We read trade association survey reports. We do not spy, however. We do not tap into their data bases, or trick their employees into giving us trade secrets, or commit any kind of espionage. Espionage is often illegal and always unethical.

Deceiving Consumers

It is permissable to persuade consumers in advertising and publicity with truthful information about research studies. It is not permissable to present information in a way that misinforms consumers. You can ask respondents to participate in a legitimate study. You should not co-opt them or hound them should they refuse to participate or quit in the middle of an interview. You should respect respondents' privacy and time. You should always be polite to respondents. Ensure that respondents do not suffer psychological harm because of the research. Protect subjects' anonymity and confidentiality. Do not ask leading or loaded questions. Do not hide or refuse to name the sponsor of the research. Never promote or sell your product under the guise of research. It is permissable to ask for personal information such as income. It is wrong to ask for other personal information not directly related to the study and the respondent's best interests. Hidden observation without consent is unethical. It is easy for an ethical researcher to observe these ethical considerations when conducting a study.

Client/Researcher Relationship

It is unethical for researchers to conduct unnecessary research or overbill a client. Researchers should not take unwarranted shortcuts to save money for themselves. They should be saving money for their client. Researchers must be careful to avoid conflicts of interest and must maintain client confidentiality.

Clients should not use researchers' proposals without compensating them for their time and ideas. Clients should always pay promptly for research services. Clients should never hide or fail to act upon information obtained in a study that uncovers anything dangerous to workers or the public. The American Marketing Association has composed a code of marketing research ethics that should be adhered to by all parties in the marketing research process.

FUTURE MARKET RESEARCH

In this book I endeavor to present alternatives to the standard marketing research text. This book is not an imitation of the twenty competing university texts, which are all the same. I do more than discuss the same topics in the same way. I address issues that are most important to current and future market research. This book was written to complement current texts. It covers areas that are skimmed over in traditional texts.

New trends in market research receive emphasis. Trends such as public information data bases, statistical software for super microcomputers, causal and predictive research that tests marketing mix variables, accurate reporting of findings, naturalistic observation, and focus groups are discussed.

I do more than describe. I make recommendations for clients and researchers to maximize quality, minimize error, and save money. I claim in the preface that this book will serve its purpose if it saves or earns money for your company. I believe it will. Refer back to specific sections when faced with research decisions. Read my recommendations. Decide. Act.

References

Aaker, D. A. (1971). *Multivariate analysis in marketing theory and application.* Belmont, CA: Wadsworth.

———, & Day, G. S. (1983). *Marketing research* (2nd ed.). New York: Wiley.

Achen, C. H. (1982). *Interpreting and using regression.* Newbury Park, CA: Sage.

Aldenderfer, M. S., & Blashfield, R. K. (1984). *Cluster analysis.* Newbury Park, CA: Sage.

Andrews, F. M., Klem, L., Davidson, T. N., O'Malley, P. M., & Rodgers, W. L. (1981). *A guide for selecting statistical techniques for analyzing social science data* (2nd ed.). Ann Arbor: University of Michigan.

Banks, S. (1965). *Experimentation in marketing.* New York: McGraw-Hill.

Barker, S. M. (1982). Find marketing data fast! *Sales and Marketing Management, 129,* 32–33.

Barr, A. J., Goodnight, J. H., Sall, J. R., and Helwig, J. T. (1976). *SAS: Statistical analysis system.* Raleigh, NC: SAS Institute.

Bean, G. J. (1988). Don't let a dominator spoil the session for everyone. *Marketing News, 22,* January 4, 6.

Bockelman, J. (1986). Electronic information gives competitive edge. *Marketing News, 20,* 24.

Brickman, G. A. (1980). Uses of voice-pitch analysis. *Journal of Advertising Research, 20,* April, 69–73.

Bush, A. J., & Hair, J. F. (1985). An assessment of the mall intercept as a data collection method. *Journal of Marketing Research, 22,* May, 158–167.

Campbell, C., & Joiner, B. L. (1973). How to get the answer without being sure you've asked the question. *The American Statistician, 27,* December, 229–231.

Campbell, D. T., & Stanley, J. C. (1963). *Experimental and quasi-experimental designs for research.* Chicago: Rand-McNally.

Charlton, P., & Ehrenberg, A. S. C. (1976). An experiment in brand choice. *Journal of Marketing Research, 13,* May, 152–160.

Cochran, W. G. (1977). *Sampling techniques.* New York: Wiley.

Cohen, J. (1977). *Statistical power analysis for the behavioral sciences* (rev. ed.). New York: Academic Press.

Cooley, W. W., & Lohnes, P. R. (1971). *Multivariate data analysis.* New York: Wiley.

Cox, K. K., & Enis, B. M. (1969). *Experimentation for marketing decisions.* Scranton, PA: International Textbook Company.

Dillon, W. R., Madden, T. J., & Firtle, N. H. (1987). *Marketing research in a marketing environment.* St. Louis: Times Mirror/Mosby College.

Dixon, W. J. (ed.). (1975). *BMDP biomedical computer programs.* Los Angeles: UCLA.

Edwards, A. L. (1968). *Experimental design in psychological research* (3rd ed.). New York: Holt.

Ferguson, G. A. (1981). *Statistical analysis in psychology and education* (5th ed.). New York: McGraw-Hill.

Flegal, D. W. (1983). How to buy marketing research. *Management Review, 72,* 63–66.

Fridlund, A. J. (1986). Statistics software. *InfoWorld,* September 1, 31–38.

Gage, T. J. (1983). Field research: Alive and well in the malls. *Advertising Age, 54,* May 23, M27–M29.

Gates, R., & Solomon, P. J. (1982). Research using the mall

intercept: State of the art. *Journal of Advertising Research, 22,* August/September, 43–49.

Gelman, E., Wang, P., Powell, B., & Smith, V. E. (1985). Hey America, Coke are it! *Newsweek,* July 22, 40–42.

Glass, G. V., McGaw, B., & Smith, M. L. (1981). *Meta-analysis in social research.* Beverly Hills: Sage.

Goldman, A. E. (1962). The group depth interview. *Journal of Marketing, 26,* July, 61–68.

Gordon, C. (1987). Taking a grassroots approach to research. *Marketing News, 21,* August 28, 22–23.

Hair, J. F., Anderson, R. E., & Tatham, R. L. (1987). *Multivariate data analysis: With readings* (2nd ed.). New York: Macmillan.

Hartley, R. F., Prough, G. E., & Flaschner, A. B. (1983). *Essentials of marketing research.* Tulsa, OK: PennWell.

Hendon, D. W. (1986). *Battling for profits.* Jonesboro, AR: Business Consultants International.

Hess, J. M. (1968). Group interviewing, in R. L. King (ed.), *New science of planning.* Chicago: American Marketing Association.

Hodges, J. C., & Whitten, M. E. (1986). *Harbrace college handbook* (10th ed.). San Diego: Harcourt Brace Jovanovich.

Huck, S. W., Cormier, W. H., & Bounds, W. G. (1974). *Reading statistics and research.* New York: Harper and Row.

Huff, D. (1954). *How to lie with statistics.* New York: Norton.

Jaffe, A. J., & Spirer, H. F. (1987). *Misused statistics: Straight talk for twisted numbers.* New York: Marcel Dekker.

Joreskog, K. G., & Sorbom, D. (1983). *LISREL VI: User's guide.* Chicago: National Educational Resources.

Karger, T. (1987). Focus groups are for focusing, and for little else. *Marketing News, 21,* August 28, 52–55.

Kim, J., & Mueller, C. W. (1978a). *Introduction to factor analysis: What it is and how to do it.* Newbury Park, CA: Sage.

———. (1978b). *Factor analysis: Statistical methods and practical issues.* Newbury Park, CA: Sage.

Kimble, G. A. (1978). *Now to use and misuse statistics.* Englewood Cliffs, NJ: Prentice-Hall.

Kinnear, T. C., & Taylor, J. R. (1987). *Marketing research: An applied approach* (3rd ed.). New York: McGraw-Hill.

Kirk, R. E. (1968). *Experimental design: Procedures for the behavioral sciences*. Belmont, CA: Brooks/Cole.

Kish, L. (1965). *Survey sampling*. New York: Wiley.

Knos, M. Z. (1986). In-depth interview can reveal what's in a name. *Marketing News, 20,* January 3, 4.

Kotler, P., & Singh, R. (1981). Marketing warfare in the 1980s. *Journal of Business Strategy,* Winter, 30–41.

Kraemer, H. C., & Thiemann, S. (1987). *How many subjects: Statistical power analysis in research*. Newbury Park, CA: Sage.

Krippendorff, K. (1980). *Content analysis: An introduction to its methodology*. Newbury Park, CA: Sage.

Kruskal, J. B., & Wish, M. (1978). *Multidimensional scaling*. Newbury Park, CA: Sage.

Labaw, P. J. (1980). *Advanced questionnaire design*. Cambridge, MA: Abt Books.

Lederhaus, M. A., & Decker, J. E. (1987). Nominal groups help identify issues and develop effective surveys. *Marketing News, 21,* August 26, 44, 48.

Lesikar, R. (1983). *Basic business communication*. Homewood, IL: Irwin.

Lewis-Beck, M. S. (1980). *Applied regression: An introduction*. Newbury Park, CA: Sage.

Lincoln, Y. S., & Guba, E. G. (1985). *Naturalistic inquiry*. Newbury Park, CA: Sage.

Linton, M., & Gallo, P. S. (1975). *The practical statistician: Simplified handbook of statistics*. Monterey, CA: Brooks/Cole.

Long, J. S. (1983). *Confirmatory factor analysis*. Newbury Park, CA: Sage.

McCarrier, J. T. (1987). Ten questions to ask when reading industry studies. *Marketing News, 21,* August 28, 5.

McGuigan, F. J. (1978). *Experimental psychology* (3rd ed.). Englewood Cliffs, NJ: Prentice-Hall.

Majors, R. E. *Communicating at work: Writing, interviewing, and speaking*. New York: Harper and Row (in press).

Malone, M. (1987). Response analyzer designed to enhance focus groups. *Marketing News, 21,* January 2, 38.

Mariampolski, H. (1984). The resurgence of qualitative research. *Public Relations Journal, 40,* July, 21–23.

_____. (1988). Ethnography makes comeback as research tool. *Marketing News, 22,* January 4, 32, 44.

Miles, M. B., & Huberman, A. M. (1984). *Qualitative data analysis: A sourcebook of new methods.* Newbury Park, CA: Sage.

Minno, J. J. (1985). Software packages for market researchers: A review. *Marketing News, 19,* September 13, 62, 67.

Monge, P. R., & Cappella, J. N. (eds.). (1980). *Multivariate techniques in human communication research.* New York: Academic Press.

Murphy, H. A., & Pick, C. E. (1980). *Effective business communications* (3rd ed.). New York: McGraw-Hill.

Nelson, R. G., & Schwartz, D. (1979). Voice-pitch analysis. *Journal of Advertising Research, 19,* October, 55–59.

Nie, N. H., Hull, G. H., Jenkins, J. G., Steinbrenner, K., & Brent, D. H. (1975). *SPSS: Statistical package for the social sciences.* New York: McGraw-Hill.

OSIRIS III. (1973). Ann Arbor: University of Michigan.

Parasuraman, A. (1986). *Marketing research.* Reading, MA: Addison-Wesley.

Payne, S. L. (1951). *The art of asking questions.* Princeton, NJ: Princeton University Press.

Peterson, R. A. (1982). *Marketing research.* Plano, TX: Business Publications.

Plutchik, R. (1974). *Foundations of experimental research* (2nd ed.). New York: Harper and Row.

Pope, J. (1980). Tips for research clients. *Advertising Age, 51,* 42.

_____. (1981). *Practical marketing research.* New York: Amacom.

Pope, J. L. (1975). 12 ways to cut marketing research costs. *Marketing News, 19,* June 6, 6.

Popper, K. R. (1959). *The logic of scientific discovery.* New York: Harper and Row.

Punj, G., & Stewart, D. W. (1983). Cluster analysis in marketing research: Review and suggestions for applications. *Journal of Marketing Research, 20,* May, 134–148.

Ray, M. L. (1973). *Unobtrusive marketing research techniques.* Cambridge, MA: Marketing Science Institute.

Roller, M. (1987). A real in-depth interview wades into the

stream of consciousness. *Marketing News, 21,* August 28, 14.

Rosenthal, R. (1984). *Meta-analytic procedures for social research.* Newbury Park: Sage.

Sackmary, B. (1985). Deciding sample size is a difficult task. *Marketing News, 19,* September 13, 30, 33.

Seymour, D. T. (1987). Seeing is believing with systematic observation. *Marketing News, 21,* August 28, 36.

Sigband, N. B., & Bateman, D. N. (1985). *Communicating in business* (2nd ed.). Glenview, IL: Scott, Foresman.

Silverstein, M. (1988). Two-way focus groups can provide startling information. *Marketing News, 22,* January 4, 31.

Smith, D. L. (1980). How to buy research services. *Public Relations Journal, 36,* 17, 20.

Soares, E. J., & Ray, L. (1986). Telephone interviewing versus paper-and-pencil self-reports: Equivalent methods to measure communication apprehension. *Communication Research Reports, 3,* December, 100–104.

Sokolow, H. (1985). In-depth interviews increasing in importance. *Marketing News, 19,* September 13, 26, 31.

Solomon, J. R., & Soares, E. J. (1987, August). Trained and naive judges' perceptions of pitch variations in English: Correlation with instrument analysis of fundamental speaking frequency. Paper presented at the 11th International Congress of Phonetic Sciences, Tallinn, Estonia, USSR.

Stern, B. L., & Crawford, T. (1986). It's time to consider certification of researchers. *Marketing News, 20,* 20–21.

Stewart, D. W. (1984). *Secondary research: Information sources and methods.* Newbury Park: Sage.

Sudman, S. (1976). *Applied sampling.* New York: Academic Press.

Tauber, E. M. (1981). Consultants: How to pick them. *Advertising Age, 52,* 527–28.

Templeton, J. F. (1987). *Focus groups.* Chicago: Probus Publishing.

Thompson, B. (1984). *Canonical correlation analysis: Uses and interpretation.* Newbury Park, CA: Sage.

Townsend, B. (1986). How to choose a consumer research company. *American Demographics, 8,* 29–34.

Treece, M. (1980). *Successful business communication* (2nd ed.). Boston: Allyn and Bacon.

Tucker, R. K., & Chase, L. J. (1980). Canonical correlation, in P. R. Monge & J. N. Cappella (eds.). *Multivariate techniques in human communication research.* New York: Academic Press.

————, Weaver, R. L., & Berryman-Fink, C. (1981). *Research in speech communication.* Englewood Cliffs, NJ: Prentice-Hall.

Webb, E. J., Campbell, D. T., Schwartz, R. D., & Sechrest, L. (1966). *Unobtrusive measures: Non-reactive research in the social sciences.* Chicago: Rand-McNally.

Weiss, K. (1987). Quantitative results possible from focus groups. *Marketing News, 20,* January 2, 33.

Weller, S. C., & Romney, A. K. (1988). *Systematic data collection.* Newbury Park, CA: Sage.

Wells, W. D., & Lo Scuito, H. A. (1966). Direct observation of purchasing behavior. *Journal of Marketing Research, 2,* August, 227.

Wheatley, K. L., & Flexner, W. A. (1987). Research tool changes the way marketers view data. *Marketing News, 21,* February 27, 23–24.

Yates, F. (1981). *Sampling methods for censuses and surveys.* New York: Macmillan.

Zikmund, W. G. (1986). *Exploring marketing research* (2nd ed.). New York: CBS College.

Index

Aaker, D.A., 123
Aaker, D.A. & Day, G.S., 83, 126, 128
Achen, C.H., 126
accuracy, 21, 43
Aldenderfer, M.S. & Blashfield, R.K., 130
Andrews, F.M., Klem, L., Davidson, T.N., O'Malley, P.M. & Rodgers, W.L., 125

Banks, S., 84, 91
Barker, S.M., 14
Barr, A.J., Goodnight, J.H., Sall, J.R., Helwig, J.T., 133
basic statistics, 117–121; functions of, 117; misuses of, 118–119; uses in data analysis, 120–121
Bean, J.G., 61

Bockelman, J., 19
Brickman, G.A., 79
Bush, A.J. & Hair, J.F., 71

Campbell, C. & Joiner, B.L., 35
Campbell, D.T. & Stanley, J.C., 83, 96–97
Charlton, P. & Ehrenberg, A.S.C., 103
cluster sample, 39
Cohen, J., 44
computer software, 114, 128, 130–136
complex experimental designs, 92–93; factorial design, 93–95; repeated measures design, 95
components of an experiment, 83

context error, 101–103
contrived observation, 75–76
control groups, 87
convenience sampling, 36
Cooley, W.W. & Lohnes,
    P.R., 123, 134
cost/benefit analysis, 4–5
Cox, K.K. & Enis, B.M., 106

data analysis, 109; analyzing
    qualitative data, 116–117;
    analyzing quantitative data,
    117–122; editing
    qualitative data, 110–111;
    editing quantitative data,
    112–115
data collection, 44; mail sur-
    vey, 47–48; personal inter-
    view, 47; telephone
    interview, 44–47
dependent multivariate tech-
    niques, 125–128
depth interviews, 51–58; pit-
    falls of, 54–57; steps in
    conducting, 57–58
design error, 96–98
Dillon, W.R., Madden, T.J. &
    Firtle, N.H., 2
Dixon, W.J., 131

editing, 110–115; qualitative
    data, 110–111; quantitative
    data, 112–115
Edwards, A.L., 107
ethics, 11, 27, 76, 148–151
ethnographic research, 70–
    73; pitfalls of, 71–73; steps
    in conducting, 73

error: context, 101–103; de-
    sign, 96–98; environment,
    100–101; experimenter,
    98–100; non-sampling, 48;
    non-response, 49; sam-
    pling, 35; time based, 89
experimentation, 81–83;
    complex designs, 92–96;
    components of, 83; design
    notation, 84–85; pitfalls of,
    96; pre-experimental de-
    signs, 91–92; quasi-experi-
    mental designs, 90–91;
    steps in conducting, 104–
    106; true experiments, 85–
    90

factorial design, 93–95
Ferguson, G.A., 120
field observation, 70–71
Flegal, D.W., 9
focus groups, 51–52, 58–68;
    analysis of, 63–64; pitfalls
    of, 60–65; recording meth-
    ods, 62–63; steps in con-
    ducting, 65–66; uses for,
    59
Fridlund, A.J., 132, 135

Gage, T.J., 71
Gantt chart, uses of, 48–49
Gates, R. & Solomon, P.J., 71
Gelman, E., Wang, P., Powell,
    B. & Smith, V.E., 99
Glass, G.V., McGaw, B. &
    Smith, M.L., 21
Goldman, A.E., 65
Gordon, C., 52, 56

Hair, J.F., Anderson, R.E. &
Tatham, R.L., 123, 126
Hartley, R.F., Prough, G.E. &
Flaschner, A.B., 2
Hendon, D.W., 148
Hess, J.M., 59
Hodges, J.C. & Whitten,
M.E., 143
Huck, S.W., Cormier, W.H.
& Bounds, W.G., 15
Huff, D., 118

interdependent multivariate
techniques, 128–130
interview: depth: 51–58;
focus groups, 51–52; per-
sonal, 47; telephone, 44–47

Jaffe, A.J. & Spirer, H.F.,
118
Joreskog, K.G. & Sorbom, D.,
134
judgment sampling, 37

Karger, T., 65
Kim, J. & Mueller, C.W., 129
Kimble, G.A., 121
Kinnear, T.C. & Taylor, J.R.,
2, 74
Kirk, R.E., 107
Kish, L., 40
Knos, M.Z., 53
Kotler, P. & Singh, R., 148
Kraemer, H.C. & Thieman,
S., 44
Krippendorff, K., 116
Kruskal, J.B. & Wish, M., 129

Labaw, P.J., 35
Lederhaus, M.A. & Decker,
J.E., 64
Lesikar, R., 143
Lewis-Beck, M.S., 126
Lincoln, Y.S. & Guba, P.G.,
80
Linton, M. & Gallo, P.S., 120
Long, J.S., 129

mail surveys, 34, 47–48
Majors, R.E., 143
Malone, M., 64
Mariampolski, H., 59, 70
marketing research: process
of, 2–3; who should do it,
5–11
McCarrier, J.T., 19
McGuigan, F.J., 107
meta-analysis, 21, 22
Miles, M.B. & Huberman,
A.M., 116
Minno, J.J., 134, 135
moderators, 60–61, 63
Monge, P.R. & Capella, J.N.,
123
monitoring equipment, 77–
79
multiple time series experiments, 91
multivariate statistics, 122–
130; dependent techniques,
125–128; general tips for
use, 124–125; interdepen-
dent techniques, 128–130;
pros & cons of, 122–124
Murphy, H.A. & Pick, C.E.,
143

Nelson, R.G. & Schwartz, D.,
    79
Nie, N.H., Hull, G.H.,
    Jenkins, J.G., Steinbrenner,
    K. & Brent, D.H., 132
non-probability sampling, 36;
    convenience, 36; judg-
    ment/expert opinion, 36,
    37; quota, 37; snowball,
    37–38
non-response error, 49
non-sampling error, 48
notation for experimentation,
    84–85

observation, 69–80; eth-
    nography, 70–73; struc-
    tured, 73–80
open ended questions, 29
OSIRIS III, 132

Parasuraman, A., 2
Payne, S.L., 35
personal interview, 47
Peterson, R.A., 2
pilot testing, 49
Plutchik, R., 121
Pope, J., 9, 30, 59, 117
Popper, K.R., 107
pre-experimental designs,
    91–92
presenting results, 142–148
probability sampling, 38–40
proposals, requests for, 9–11
Punj, G. & Stewart, D.W.,
    130

qualitative data analysis, 116–
    117

quantitative data analysis,
    117–122
quasi-experimental designs,
    90–91
question development, 29–
    31; asking difficult ques-
    tions, 33–35; number for-
    mats, 30–31; open/closed
    ended, 29–30; phrasing,
    30; scaling, 31–33
questionnaire construction,
    27; format, 27–29; pream-
    ble, 28
quota sampling, 37

Ray, M.L., 80
random assignment, 88
random sampling, 38; area,
    39; cluster, 39; multistage,
    40; simple, 38, 40; strat-
    ified, 39; systematic, 39
repeated measures design, 95
request for proposal, 9–11
reporting results, 137; pre-
    sentation delivery, 146–
    148; presentation prepara-
    tion, 142–146; report ap-
    pearance, 138–139; report
    format, 139–142; reporting
    statistics, 118–121
Roller, M., 56
Rosenthal, R., 21

Sackmary, B., 42
sampling, 35; choosing a
    method, 40; error, 38;
    frame, 46; non-probability,
    36–38; probability, 38–40;
    size, 41–44

secondary data, 4, 13–14; pros & cons, 14–15; sources of, 15–22
Seymour, D.T., 77
Sigband, N.B. & Bateman, D.N., 143
Silverstein, M., 64
Smith, D.L., 9
Soares, E.J. & Ray, L., 33, 45
software, 114, 128, 130–136
Sokolow, H., 52
Solomon Four design, 88–90
Solomon, J.R. & Soares, E.J., 41, 79
Stern, B.L. & Crawford, T., 9
Stewart, D.W., 15
structured observation: contrived, 75–76; direct/indirect, 74–75; disguised/undisguised, 75; pitfalls of, 76–80; steps in conducting, 80
Sudman, S., 40
surveying, 25–50; data collection, 44–50; ethics of, 27; mall, 34, 47–48; questionnaire construction, 27–35; when to do it, 26–27
syndicated research, 22; pros & cons, 22–23

Tauber, E.M., 9
telephone interview, 44–47

Templeton, J.F., 66
Thompson, B., 126
time series design, 88
Townsend, B., 9
Treece, M., 143
true experiments, 85–90; after only, 85; before and after, 88; control groups, 87; Solomon Four, 88–90
Tucker, R.K. & Chase, L.J., 126
Tucker, et al., 102–103, 129

visual aids, 118, 142, 144–145

Webb, E.J., Campbell, D.T., Schwartz, R.D. & Sechrest, L., 80
Weiss, K., 64
Weller, S.C. & Romney, A.K., 80
Wells, W.D. & Lo Scuito, H.A., 80
Wheatley, K.L. & Flexner, W.A., 64

Yates, F., 40

Zikmund, W.G., 2

About the Author

ERIC J. SOARES is Associate Professor of Marketing at California State University, Hayward. He has done cost-effective research consulting with more than 20 small and medium-sized firms and is President of Tsunami Products, a sea kayak manufacturing firm.